BREAKING FREE FROM DESTRUCTIVE RELATIONSHIPS

*An Overcomer's Guide:
Freedom from Controlling,
Manipulative & Domineering
People in the Church*

Lynda L. Patrick

Lighthouse Publications

Unless otherwise indicated, Bible quotations are taken from the
King James Version.

Author's Contact Information
Lynda L. Patrick
Power House Intl. Ministries
P.O. Box 53323
Cincinnati, OH 45253
(888) 221-5887
LyndaPatrick@PowerHse.org
www. PowerHse.org

Publisher
Lighthouse Publications
2028 Larkin Avenue
Elgin, IL 60123
(847) 697-6788
www.Lighthouse-Publications.com

Cover Design
Scott Wallis & Associates
2028 Larkin Avenue
Elgin, IL 60123
(847) 468-1457
www.ScottWallis.net

Dedication

To my daughters,
Teresa, Jocelyn, & Kiana,

Who were eyewitnesses to the abuse,
partakers in the suffering,
and destined to walk in "HIS"
manifested glory.

I love you dearly.
Mom

Foreword

When the mind has been enslaved from its legitimate rights, privileges and power in the Kingdom dimension, manipulation and human control are not far behind. When one's own authority has been turned against him/herself, that life is now considered a puppet in the hands of those who claim to "be authority from God."

In this book, Lynda Patrick explains the facets of spiritual control and abuse, a thing that so many believers have faced and *are still facing*. She gives insights into the beginnings of abuse and the codependent outcomes that are produced from it. She also articulates the remedies of the Spirit that will once again "set free the mind and the spirit to embrace, believe and soar into the eternal purposes that were predetermined by the Father before the abuse even took place."

She gives practical insight into the process of mental and spiritual freedoms that, if applied and believed, will create a new realm of wholeness for the reader. Increase of the Spirit is already present. You do not have to be the victim of "false authorities or false leaderships." You do not have to be "your own victim, as well."

Freedom is in you. Now is the time for it to be withdrawn from you as a mighty river. Enjoy this book of freedom.

Dr. Undrai Fizer
Exploring the Vision Ministries International
Kairos' Life Technologies

Preface

This book is designed to share with its readers the practical and painfully necessary steps that ensure a victorious, abundant life for survivors of spiritual witchcraft. The popularity of "how to" books and "step" programs normally would cause me to shy away from proclaiming that there are steps to being free. However, I must admit, because of my own experience and the experiences of others, there are undeniable stages in the process of becoming free that need to be shared.

There are no time limits or formulas being offered. By unction of the Holy Spirit, I do believe that these insights will help all seekers of freedom to identify landmarks and barriers. I offer these insights with the effective power that accompanies "having been there and done that." I have, along with many others, come up out of the trash heap to become a declarer of truth with a mandate to show others that there is life after religion. It is my expressed prayer that in so doing, light will shine in darkness and overcome it.

Contents

Introduction

Manipulation is exercised in every facet of human relationships. It is something we learn as children. Initially a baby cries, as its only means of communication. By the age of 2 or 3, children have developed a small vocabulary and know how to ask for what they want. At this point, you can observe a change in "how" they use crying. A child asks for a piece of candy. Your answer is "no" or "not now." The child begins to cry and you change your answer to "okay." You have been manipulated.

All over the world, we are inundated with commercials, cleverly designed to manipulate us into buying products that we neither want nor need. Through guilt, our teenagers manipulate their way into the driver's seat of our car after we have made a solemn oath that they would not have an opportunity to wreck our vehicle. The soap operas are excellent examples of manipulation, control, intimidation and witchcraft at its best. Day in and day out, a myriad of individuals entertain us by seeing who can be the most manipulative and get away with it.

In the work place, in our homes and in our churches, these spirits operating through people consistently approach us. No one group, nation or race has a monopoly on this problem. My personal experience has been far-reaching. From the traditional Methodist, to today's non-denominational/interdenominational charismatic, spiritual witchcraft thrives. Through the voice of family members who know exactly what you should do with your life, to your prayer partner who also knows exactly what you should do with your life, the spirit of Jezebel speaks forth its agenda.

The burning of candles, reciting incantations and having séances are not the only manifestations of witchcraft. These things are usually what people visualize when they hear the term "witchcraft." Controlling and manipulating people, using fear and intimidation to secure our own will without regard to the will of others, is also witchcraft. There is something about our ego that makes it difficult for us to admit that we have been manipulated or deceived. There is the temptation to play it off by calling it something else. In order to move into the fullness of what God has for our lives, we must embrace the truth of where we are and how we relate to people. Once we make a commitment to know the truth, making the necessary changes will propel us into destiny.

Whenever an individual purposes to confront spirits of control and manipulation, they will encounter roots that are both deep and interwoven. In recent years, the Holy Spirit has brought illumination to this root system. As a result of this illumination, we are now able to clearly see the connection between **control, manipulation, the spirit of Jezebel and spiritual witchcraft**. There is no aspect of our lives that escapes the diabolical detriment of these ancient spirits. Cloaked in religion, tradition, and legalism, the spirit of Jezebel thrives in our earnest desire to please God. Lately there has been much written about Jezebel, I believe by design of the Holy Spirit.

The Body of Christ has had to invest time and energy into unlearning things like *blind faith, achieving righteousness through works, etc.,* so that we might be able to embrace other things such as *how to receive progressive truth, fresh revelation and <u>now</u> obedience.* Being a Jezebel or under the influence of the spirit of Jezebel has nothing to do with the wearing of lipstick, or jewelry or indecent clothes. It does have to do with; *the usurping and misuse of power or authority; a tenacious opposition to God by opposing His prophets; and the gaining of the* *ear of authority or leadership through control and manipulation.*

Because the spirit of Jezebel is very subtle, we are often in situations where we are being controlled and manipulated, and we are not even aware of it. Spiritual witchcraft is the manipulation of a person's will through religious practices. In other words, it is the holding captive of a person through traditions and doctrines of men, camouflaged as holiness, spiritual superiority, elitism, special revelations and sanctification. Relationship and intimacy with the Lord Jesus Christ is replaced with a well-defined list of "do's and don'ts." Using what amounts to brainwashing techniques, new converts are slowly and easily pulled in. If you have been drawn to this book and are experiencing some of these symptoms, consider the possibility of the presence of spiritual witchcraft.

1. Feeling trapped in your spiritual relationships

2. Frustrated with your own spiritual growth

3. Feeling connected to God only through your leadership

4. Looking for spiritual acceptance from those around you

5. Trying to maintain your right standing with God through works

6. Having a constant fear of backsliding

7. Having a fear of disapproval from God if you leave your church or religious organization

8. Confused about your purpose or call

9. Having trouble discerning between the will of God for your life and the will of others

It is important to note here that none of these in and by themselves means that you are under the influence of spiritual witchcraft. However, the presence of a combination of these things should provoke you to consider the possibility of the presence of spiritual witchcraft. For example, you might be confused about your purpose or call (#8). That doesn't mean your pastor is a witch or warlock. As we take in the whole picture under the guidance of the Holy Spirit, we will be able to know exactly what is happening in our spiritual lives. The end of each chapter has been designed to help you identify "landmarks" (behavior, mindset, or experiences), "barriers" (stumbling/road blocks), and solutions (steps or remedies). I have also included prayers and scriptural support.

• Introduction •

SECTION ONE

"O Foolish Galatians, who hath bewitched you, that ye should not obey the truth, before whose eyes Jesus Christ hath been evidently set forth, crucified among you?"

Galatians 3:1

Chapter One

Getting Out

Admit It

L etting in the truth about our experiences, the dynamics of our interpersonal relationships, and all the council of the Godhead are essential for growth. And growth is what God desires. Do you remember how awkward and embarrassing it was during your teenage years to admit that you had a crush on someone?

During the fifties and sixties, puberty was something that many of us would have liked to skip. Growing up during that time seemed to be filled with one embarrassing situation after another. The changes in our bodies, our emotions, and other people's expectations all contributed to our desire for quick arrival into adulthood. Some of that same awkwardness can be present in our spiritual lives as we embrace the call to maturity. Admitting the truth about anything of which we would rather not talk or think can be challenging. When Jesus encountered the woman at the well, she didn't volunteer any truth about her personal life. She engaged in a religious conversation. She was telling Jesus all about worship (Please read John 4:6-29 in order to refresh your memory of this story).

However, when she was confronted with "truth" as it related to her personal life, she was able to see, recognize and benefit from the truth that was being presented. In Matthew 8:32, Jesus said, "And you shall know the truth and the truth shall make you free." As we study the Word of God and allow His principles to become our guide for living, we will have to make many adjustments. Our habits, ways of thinking and relationships will undergo many changes as we embrace what His Word declares to be right and acceptable for the lifestyle of a believer. At some point, we must move from *"WHY is this happening to me?"* and a need to lay blame, into *"what do I do NOW?"* Admitting where you are is the bridge that will bring you out. Understanding *HOW* it happened will become preventive medicine for the future.

"Behold I stand at the door, and knock: if any man hear My voice, and open the door, I will come in to him, and will sup with him and he with Me" (Rev. 3:20). If you open up, if you _admit Me_, I will come in. "I am the Way, the Truth and the Life: no man cometh unto the Father but by Me" (John 14:6). _Admit_ the truth! Letting Jesus in also requires letting in the truth about our lives, our hidden secrets, our fears, etc. If we are born-again, it is because of our ability to _admit_ we were sinners in need of a savior. "For all have sinned, and come short of the glory of God" (Rom. 3:23). It is the work of the Holy Spirit to reveal. "Howbeit when He, the Spirit of truth, is come, He will guide you into all truth: for He shall not speak of himself; but whatsoever He shall hear, that shall He speak: and He will show you things to come" (John 16:13).

The Holy Spirit speaks to our hearts and to our minds. He speaks to us by bringing a passage of Scripture to our conscious minds, or He might speak through a minister on the radio. His voice can also be heard in something a child might say. For example, one day I was riding in the car with my daughter and five-year-old granddaughter. I can't recall how the conversation began, because my granddaughter is quite talkative. But, she began to tell her mother how she came to be with us. She said that God had sent her down from heaven. She continued, "God knew that you needed someone, so He put me in your belly." From time to time, she has shared many other insights with us that are far beyond her years as it relates to understanding. I believe the Holy Spirit was using her to speak words of comfort to her mother at a time when she really needed to hear them.

There are many other examples of ways that the Holy Spirit speaks to us in our everyday lives. It is important not to limit His access to our spiritual ears. Expecting to hear from Him only through the Sunday morning message limits the amount of revelation that He is able to give us. He has been given to us as a Gift, a Teacher, a Comforter, a Guide and a Friend. We must become and remain open, empowering Him to work more freely in our hearts. When He is allowed to work freely, He will reveal. We must validate the presence of the Holy Spirit in our lives by allowing the "Truth" He presents or reveals to supersede all other "truths." Being able to receive His insight is a necessary skill for enjoying all that Jesus has obtained for us through His suffering, death, burial and resurrection.

Getting Out

For 18 years, I belonged to the Holiness movement. I got saved and came up through the ranks, so to speak. I eventually became a pastor and traveled, establishing several churches in different states on the East Coast. During the time that I was a member of this organization, I submitted to many with whom I did not necessarily agree. The strength of my conviction was that, as long as I was a member, I was obligated to obey the rules. The day came when, as a pastor, I could no longer teach and enforce those rules. I had to leave. I did not realize at that time that God was the Author of my discontent, and I struggled.

At the center of my inner turmoil was unwillingness on my part to be separated from my spiritual mother. This woman of God, my pastor's wife, had been very instrumental in my spiritual growth. God had used her to help me to be able to forgive my father. She taught me how to pray. She helped me to answer the call of God on my life. I faced head-on a battle between my love for her and my desire to be free. Somewhere in my subconscious mind and in my spirit, I knew that God was offering me more than what I was experiencing. In 1988, I took a difficult but bold step. I resigned from the pastorate, took a sabbatical from organized religion, and unknowingly embarked on a course that has literally taken me around the world.

I had to face some very difficult "truths," the most difficult being that for all of my spiritual life I had been controlled, manipulated and owned by an organization and not by the Holy Spirit. It was only after I got out that God began to show me why, how, and what had happened to me. I did not "throw the baby out with the bath water." I learned self-discipline, commitment, loyalty and how to fast and pray; things that are priceless to me now. But, I must _admit_ that, during that time or season in my life, they were all misdirected. There is no doubt that God uses people. But how we relate to people is still to be by direction of the Holy Spirit. People change, and how we relate to them also must reflect change. It was tough in the beginning, but my relationship with my spiritual mother survived, and we remained close until she went home to be with the Lord. There are relationships that will last a lifetime and relationships that are for seasons. It is important to be able to discern the difference.

Getting out from under the influence of spiritual witchcraft requires a commitment to remain true to God at all cost. We must be willing to separate people and our relationships with them from *How* we feel about them. In other words, we are commanded to love. We must love everyone, but we do not have to submit to those who abuse us. We do not have to give them open access to speak into our spirits. We must understand God's use of seasons and timings. Critical to our quest to become free is a genuine assessment of how we handle change. Whether it is a change of season, God's timing or a change in a relationship, how you respond to the need for change will directly impact your ability to become free.

If you are under the influence of spiritual witchcraft, you have been victimized. How you became victimized is addressed in *Chapter Four, Victim Thinking and Denial*. No one chooses to become a victim of any kind, but once you _admit_ that you have been victimized, you must choose to end the abuse. There are certain characteristics that can make us more vulnerable to becoming victims. A closer look at some of these characteristics, such as *CHILD-LIKE FAITH, BLIND FAITH, SIBLING RIVALRY* and *OUR NEED FOR ACCEPTANCE,* will give us greater understanding in our quest to be free.

Now, let us examine some of the things that might have opened the door for spiritual witchcraft to creep into our lives. If we can see and accept the _how_ of what has happened to us, we will be better equipped to ensure that it never happens again.

Landmark: Has the Holy Spirit been speaking to you about change? Do you have any relationships that you _know_ are not beneficial to you? Is there any _truth_ to which you have closed your eyes? Do you find yourself longing for more spiritually? Are you growing in your relationship with the Lord? Have you identified the presence of controlling or manipulating influences in your life? Do you have a sense of liberty in your spirit?

Barriers: Being fearful of change. Not wanting to come out of a comfort zone. Not being totally honest with ourselves or being religious in our thinking or mindset. Not having an open mind. Not being open to receive fresh revelation of the Word of God.

Solution: If there is the presence of any spiritual witchcraft in your lives, you must admit it and *GET OUT* from under it! Your desire to be rightly connected to God must be greater than any allegiance to any relationship you have here on earth. Getting out is not limited to leaving a church or an organization. You might only need to sever your relationship with one individual as opposed to leaving your church. People exercise spiritual witchcraft. Getting out will require letting go of relationships. Depending on how you are related to the person controlling or manipulating you, change may be required in different ways. To know what to change or where change is necessary will require input from the Holy Spirit and honesty on your part with yourself.

Prayer: Father, in Jesus' Name, I come to You acknowledging my need of Your grace and mercy. Lord I look to You as my Shepherd. I confess all my sins to You, asking for and accepting Your forgiveness. Let the Blood of Jesus wash over my mind, my heart and my spirit. Lord, I am Yours. You are my Master and my Savior. My allegiance is to You, and I will have no other God before You. I hear the voice of the Good Shepherd, and it is His voice only that I choose to obey.

Holy Spirit, speak to my mind and my heart with clarity. Let the Light shine in darkness. Bring into the open everything that is hidden. Lord, I embrace Your purpose for my life. Help me to walk into destiny. Dismantle anything that has been wrongly built upon the foundation that You have laid in my life. Father, with my whole heart, soul, mind and with all of my strength I desire to bring glory and honor to You. Thank You, Lord, for change. Thank You for victory, and thank You for liberty. In Jesus' Name, I pray, Amen.

Scripture Helps: I have not given you the verses, read the entire chapter to help you get a good understanding: Psalm 1, 18, 37; Proverbs 3, 14; Ecclesiastes 3; Isaiah 43; Matthew 10, 11, 13, 16; Luke 10; John 14, 16; 2 Thessalonians 3; Revelation 2.

Chapter Two

Childlike Faith vs. Blind Faith

Child-Like Faith

It was a glorious day when I rededicated my life to the Lord. I accepted the Lord as my personal Savior in 1969, just two months before I left home for my freshman year at college. I had only been saved a short time when I arrived in Worcester, Massachusetts, and many new things awaited me there. I was not used to freedom, and it didn't take long for me to forget about my new relationship with the Lord. A more accurate assessment might be that I went buck wild. In 1971, through some God ordained circumstances, I came to my senses and during spring break I visited my mother's new church. My experience that day was very much like the church scene in the movie, THE COLOR PURPLE.

There was much crying, repenting and joyful shouts of "Hallelujah!" for the wayward child who had come home. Even though I had many new worldly experiences during those two years in college, I was very much a "newborn" child of God. I was raised in a Methodist church, and I knew nothing of Pentecostals or Holiness churches. My new church was a Holiness church, and I was the best kind of new convert – a naïve one. As we continue, you will better understand how new to the faith I really was.

In Matthew 18:3, Jesus addresses the importance of becoming like children in order to enter the kingdom of heaven. "Verily I say unto you, except ye be converted, and become as little children, ye shall not enter into the kingdom of heaven." Jesus' teaching confirms why and how spiritual newborns are so vulnerable; they are susceptible spiritually just like natural newborn babies are naturally. As it is in the natural, so it is in the spirit. Because of this, there are things that we know about newborns from which we can gain insight. These insights will be formidable weapons in our battle to be free.

1. Newborns are totally dependent upon some adult or caretaker(s), usually the biological parents.

2. Newborns are vulnerable and need protection.

3. Newborns do not, by nature, feel the need to be protected from those who have given them life.

4. Newborns are not capable of meeting their own needs.

5. Newborns do not feel responsible for meeting their own needs.

6. Newborns do not question the presence or absence of wisdom in their parents or caregivers.

7. Newborns are innocent.

This list is not in anyway conclusive, but it will get us to the point. When a baby is conceived in the womb, it is enclosed in a protective, nurturing environment. Once the baby has been born, there is a continuing need for that which once was provided internally to be provided externally. God's order for the natural is for a parental team (mother, father, extended family members) to continue to provide for their new dependent. Babies arrive in this world as totally dependent children and must be taught to be independent adults.

As we trace the natural birth process, we gain a better understanding of what God desires in His relationship with us. Before we are born-again, we exist in a protective, nurturing environment provided by God. We eat His food, breathe His air, and enjoy His life. Genesis 2:7 says, "And the Lord God formed man of the dust of the ground, and breathed into his nostrils the breath of life; and man became a living soul." Matthew 5:45 says, "That ye may be the children of your Father which is in heaven: for He maketh His sun to rise on the evil and on the good, and sendeth rain on the just and on the unjust." After we are born-again, the Godhead team (Father, Son and Holy Spirit) continues to provide for their new dependent. We arrive into the kingdom of God as independent adults, and must be taught to be dependent children of God.

The presence of these qualities in new believers is most desirable and necessary. Every new born-again believer should feel this way about God the Father, God the Son, and God the Holy Spirit – our life-giving parents. Eternal life is the gift of God, paid for by the Son and dispersed by the Spirit to whomsoever will receive it. God reserves for Himself the right and privilege of being called FATHER: Matthew 23:9 says, "And call no man your father upon the earth: for One is your Father, which is in heaven." God has chosen to use people to reconcile the world to Him. 2 Corinthians 5:18 says, "And all things are of God, who hath reconciled us to Himself by Jesus Christ, and hath given to us the ministry of reconciliation." We must keep those whom He uses in their rightful place. No matter how people are connected to our lives, *child-like faith* is reserved for God and God alone.

As a precious, vulnerable, new born-again believer, you should be latched on to the breast of Jesus at birth. The importance of making sure that new believers are connected to God and not to people can also be seen in what happens when a baby at birth is given a bottle before the breast. I was recently an eyewitness to such an occasion. The birth mother had indicated her intention to breast-feed. During the examination of the baby, there was concern for some irregular breathing and the baby was placed in the special care unit for observation.

When the baby was being moved, the maternal grandmother reminded the nurse that the baby was to be breast-fed. The grandmother specifically asked the nurse to inform those who would be caring for the baby of the mother's desire to breast-feed. The baby remained in the special care unit for about four hours. During that time, the baby was given a bottle. The baby was then brought to the mother's room. At the next feeding time, the mother tried to breast feed, but the baby would not latch on and had to be given a bottle. From this experience, we can see the importance of making sure that new converts are linked directly to God, through Jesus, by the power of the Holy Spirit. Regardless of our spiritual ages, *WE NEED TO BE CONNECTED TO GOD, PERIOD.*

A good indication that you are wrongly connected to any person is an inability to hear God for yourself. If all of your answers to your life situations come from other people, you are not as connected to God as you should be. If you experience anxiety at the thought of sharing with someone what you believe God is telling you to do, you might not be rightly connected. If you need someone else's permission before obeying God, check your connections. There should be a difference between sharing with your leader the vision God has placed in your heart and feeling that you need his or her permission to carry out that vision. The sharing of information should be for the purpose of seeing how God would have you come together, or to determine if there is a place of agreement for the vision. The absence of agreement alone does not mean either party has missed God. It could be an issue of timing. But, when you come away from that time of sharing, you should be encouraged to go further with God – not discouraged.

Soul Ties

Another name for the connection between two or more people is _soul ties_. Soul ties are cords or the connection that bind us to an individual in the soul realm. The soul realm consists of what we think, what we feel and what we choose. Often, soul ties are thought of as only having to do with romantic involvement. In reality, soul ties are established in most relationships. David and Jonathan are a good example of soul ties. They were bound together so strongly that only death could separate them. Therefore, not all soul ties are bad or undesirable. Amos 3:3 says, "Can two walk together, except they be agreed?" What is the place of agreement between you and those with whom you walk?

To determine the origin of our soul ties, we need to examine _what_ binds us to the other person. Are we connected because of divine purpose? Does it promote spiritual growth in each other? Is there mutual respect, or is the relationship one-sided? Does our soul tie to an individual cause us to cross any boundaries? For example, as two Christian women in a sister-to-sister relationship, do we find ourselves role-playing as man and woman? Or, if you are my brother in the Lord, do you respond to me, a woman, as a husband might? Right relationships will line up with God's law and will produce righteous fruit. The most important and effective tool to ensure that we are not drawn into spiritual witchcraft is to allow the Holy Spirit to both examine and adjust our relationships.

Because of the innate power within soul ties, when separating ourselves from people or an organization, it is sometimes difficult to discern whether separation is what God desires or what we desire. A measuring rod that I have learned to use is the absence of peace. Whenever I receive direction, instruction or correction that I believe is from God, I also receive the peace of God. Even when what is being required is not what I want to hear, it is still engulfed in a great peace. Of course, first and foremost, the communication must agree with the Word of God and be Scripturally sound.

In addition, through the years, I have learned that what God requires of me is always accompanied with His grace. Sometimes I have to verbally accept and apply that grace, but when He is doing the talking, His grace always abounds. If you are struggling or in turmoil about a directive or instruction, ask God to confirm Himself as the Source of what you are hearing. If His peace is not present, then ask the Holy Spirit to show you why you are not at peace. Ask very specific questions. He will give you specific answers. When did you first notice that your peace was gone? What were the circumstances or events surrounding the departure of your peace? Don't be afraid to ask the hard questions. Do you force yourself to attend your church or to be around certain individuals? If so, why? How will you know when change is necessary? Breaking soul-ties is a painful procedure that you will be able to endure because of the peace of God.

In sharing with people who are fearful of coming out of spiritually abusive relationships, I have heard the following reasoning more than once. I would like to address it here. It has been said, "God wouldn't tell me to leave where I am without giving me some place new to go." This is not exactly true. First of all, it is dangerous to put

God in a box. We are all different. God recognizes our differences. His interactions with us reflect that He honors those differences.

Secondly, throughout the Bible we see illustrations of times when God gave instructions that required faith for the person being instructed to obey God (Abraham, Moses, Gideon). "We walk by faith and not by sight" (2 Cor. 5:7). Rather than focusing on the next instruction, you must get the NOW instruction. What is God saying to you, now? Seek Him, purpose to hear Him, and then obey. Your only reason for getting out must be your conviction that God is telling you that now is the time to leave. When you encounter the hard places because of your choice to obey Him, knowing that God told you to leave will produce the grace that you need to walk in obedience.

Blind Faith

I arrived into the kingdom of God full of joy, wonder and amazement. I was happy to be at peace with God, and looked forward to what lay ahead. I had absolutely no suspicion or expectation that life would be anything other than marvelous with my new church family. Whenever the church door opened, which was very often, I was there. Let me share a typical week, and you will agree that I was very committed to my new family.

- Sunday School – 9:30 AM

- Sunday Morning Service – 11:00 AM until about 2:00 PM (depending on how testimony service went)

- HYPU OR YPI – 6:00 PM (Holiness Young People's Union & Young People's Institute)

- Sunday Evening Service – 7:30 PM

- Tuesday Night Service – 8:00 PM

- Friday Night Bible Study – 8:00 PM (after fasting all day and not eating until service ended at about 11:00 PM)

- Saturday Night "Joy Night" Service 8:00 PM until …

- Scheduled choir rehearsals and other meetings were woven into this permanent schedule.

The real noteworthy observation in regard to this schedule is the fact that attendance was not optional. To miss any one of these services would be cause for public repentance, because of being in a backslidden condition. Did I know any

27

better? No. I was the trusting new born-again believer. I did not question anything my leaders said in those days. I accepted everything as *this is the way it is* or *normal* – how about you? I now know that at that time in my spiritual walk with the Lord, I had an abundance of *blind faith*.

Misplaced trust, loyalty, fear, intimidation and commitment to people instead of God forge together, creating *blind faith*, making it almost impossible for truth to get in and the victim (me, in this case) to get out. Now the term *blind faith* could easily be considered an oxymoron. An oxymoron is a term or phrase that takes two opposing ideas and puts them together (for example, cruel kindness). Because of our understanding of what faith is ("Now faith is the substance of things hoped for, the evidence of things not seen," Heb. 11:1), we could ask the question, "How can there be such a thing as blind faith?"

Blind faith believes in something or someone without any regard as to whether or not that faith is earned or substantiated. For instance, it is natural for us to have faith and trust in those who hold offices of authority. It is a part of our social experience to trust teachers, policemen, and ministers. We have blind faith in our parents.

We must have a negative or harmful experience to lose our trust or faith in our parents, siblings or other family members. This transfers very easily to our spiritual experiences. From the time we are born-again, we encounter and establish relationships that should be full of trust. It is devastating to find ourselves in situations in which that trust is violated. It is even far more difficult to admit that someone we trusted, and should have been able to trust, has deceived us.

Our faith in individuals must not go beyond the Christ in them. We must put our faith, not "blindly" but attentively, in the fruit that we are able to see. Apostle Paul prayed "that the eyes of our understanding be enlightened" (Eph. 1:18). We need to see in order to understand who we are and what God desires for us as believers. The Word of God gives us the conditions and sets the standard for how we are to relate to our leaders and those in authority.

Hebrews 13:7 (*Amplified*) says, "Remember your leaders and superiors in authority [for it was they] who brought to you the Word of God. Observe attentively and consider their manner of living (the outcome of their well-spent lives) and imitate their faith (their conviction that God exists and is the Creator and Ruler of all things, the

Provider and Bestower of eternal salvation through Christ, and their leaning of the entire human personality on God in absolute trust and confidence in His power, wisdom, and goodness)."

So, here Paul says that when it comes to our leaders, we must keep our eyes open, see and respond appropriately. This can only be done effectively through personal knowledge of the Word of God. As we give ourselves to diligent study of His Word, the Holy Spirit will give us clarity and greater understanding. We do not put our faith in the person, but rather in the God within the person.

We must put our faith and trust in God and His Word, and that faith is to have the last say. We also must not go past the red flags. As we keep our eyes open, we are going to see things that will require a response from us. In my own experience, there were signs that should have caused me to question and or leave that particular church much sooner than I actually did. But, I chose to excuse or rationalize away anything that I saw that was an indication that my leaders were human beings, capable of making mistakes and capable of being off in their teachings.

Having blind faith in people opens the door to seducing spirits. To seduce means to entice or to lead away. Seducing spirits are expressly sent out to find any available entrance into your life. We must be attentive to allow the Holy Spirit to work any negative characteristics out of us, preventing the enemy from having a way to lead us astray. The enemy looks for character flaws or areas where the <u>truth</u> of God's Word has not been applied, and he works a strategic plan to pull you away from your purpose and destiny in God. If we are full of self-ambition, or have a thirst for power, or are over-zealous or still have greed or lust, then the devil has found a way to deceive and entice us.

In the early years of my involvement in my new church family, one open door in my life was rebellion. I did not want to preach. I wanted no part of the ministry. So, the enemy sent people into my path who portrayed a picture of God as mean and willful. They didn't tell me that with loving-kindness He would draw me into purpose. They proclaimed Him to be as they were. It was, "you are going to do this, Lynda, because I said so. This is the rule." This, in turn, gave free reign for my stubbornness to manifest. Spirits use people. When we blindly put our faith in people, we open the door to be broadsided by the enemy. We expect the devil to use sinners. We do not expect him to use anyone who is professing salvation.

If we have blind faith in people, it is possible and very likely that we also have blind faith in ourselves. If we refuse to open our eyes to our own weaknesses or shortcomings, we will be less willing to see weaknesses in others. I don't seem to be able to emphasize enough the reality of this one point. *Love is not lost at the admittance of someone's weakness or shortcoming.* Just look at how we relate to our children or other family members. We live with their weakness everyday.

I don't love my daughter any less because she is quick-tempered. It doesn't take anything away from my love to be able to say she has a short temper. Actually the Word of God teaches that "love covers a multitude of sins" (1 Pet. 4:8). This is not ostrich-like stick-your-head-in-the-sand coverage. It is "speak the truth in love" coverage, because *the truth you know and accept* sets free. Failing to see and accept people as they are gives access to the spirit of Jezebel, who will endeavor to control and manipulate us. This is accomplished through deception. If you cannot receive the truth as presented by the Holy Spirit, then you are making an announcement that you are open and available to be deceived.

I remember one event specifically that was devastating to me personally. There was a particular evangelist in our congregation, whom I held in very high esteem. Through different people, the Holy Spirit tried to give me insight that would have put her on a more human level and not the pedestal that I had built for her. I refused this insight with declarations ranging from not wanting to be judgmental to accusing others of being jealous. In my refusal to accept His insights, I opened the door to the enemy.

When the truth finally came crashing in on me, I was devastated. I had been deceived, but the impact of that deception would have been much different had I accepted the truth the Holy Spirit was trying to reveal. Instead of being able to intercede for her, I was somewhere licking my wounds and having an experience that would teach me in the future to turn my head the other way and to *mind my own business*.

Landmark: Do you have child-like faith in anyone other than God? Are there any people in your life that you do not question? Are there people in your life that you respect just because of their title? Are you able to see fruit in the lives of the people to whom you submit? Do you have blind faith in anyone? If so, what does God want you to do about it?

Barriers: Justifying or rationalizing will hinder you from being able to transfer dependence upon people to dependence upon God. Not examining soul ties will stop you from entering into all that God has for you.

Solution: Being honest with yourself and God is often the key to a breakthrough. Ask the Holy Spirit to reveal any relationships that do not line up with the Word of God. Be thorough. Admit to yourself the truth of the presence of any controlling, manipulating relationships. Don't just talk about it, take the necessary steps to get out of any and all spiritually abusive situations. Cut every soul tie through prayer. Blind faith in people or religious institutions should be replaced with faith in God. Romans 10:17 says, "Faith cometh by hearing and hearing by the Word of God." It is up to you. "Building yourselves up on your most holy faith" (Jude 20). You must open your eyes, your ears and your heart to the Word of God, which will build up your faith.

Prayer: Father, thank You for Your grace upon my life. Thank You for loving me. I thank You, Lord, for the faith that You have placed in my heart. Lord, my eyes are upon You. Holy Spirit, I invite You to search me. Search my heart and my mind. Bring to my attention anything or person I might be trusting in other than You. Father, I use the authority You have given me, and by faith I cut, sever and break every soul tie that is not pleasing to You. Jesus, I restore You to Your rightful place in my heart and in my life.

I thank You, Lord, for relationships that are established according to Your purpose for my life. I release all relationships that do not bring glory to Your Name. Father, set me free from the spirit of Jezebel, and any controlling, manipulating influences in my life in Jesus' Name. Holy Spirit, ignite my heart once again and let faith arise. As I meditate on Your Word, let faith come into my heart. I open my mind and my heart to You and to the truth of Your Word. I ask You to strengthen me and continue to let the truth of Your Word transform my mind. In Jesus' Name I pray, Amen.

Scripture Helps: Psalm 20; Amos 3; Habakkuk 2; Matthew 9, 16, 17, 18, 19, 21; Mark 10, 11; Luke 5, 8, 17, 22; Romans 1, 8, 12; James 2; Jude.

Chapter Three

Sibling Rivalry – and Needing to Be Accepted

Sibling Rivalry

There is no doubt in my mind that the acceptance of my new environment as "normal" was re-enforced by the presence of others (older siblings in the faith) who also towed the line. The Holiness church I had joined was a "movement" or a denomination, having believers in our local assembly as well as throughout the United States. We had one church in California, several in the West Indies, and approximately 300 churches scattered up and down the East Coast and as far west as Chicago. These churches were divided into districts. There were three presiding bishops, and the districts were divided equally between them. Each district also had a "ruling elder." Many years passed by before I really understood how things worked. In those days, it was common practice to learn the rules and abide by them. A book referred to as *The Discipline* was a compilation of our rules along with the supporting Scriptures. I will share in more detail some of those rules in *Chapter Ten,* MOVING OUT OF RELIGION AND INTO RELATIONSHIP. The sad truth of the matter is that I did not question or consider that there was anything amiss or wrong. I was happy to obey and submit to those who ruled over me; after all, I was the new kid on the block.

Anyone who has been blessed with more than one child will be able to attest to the reality of influential power that is executed by the firstborn over all who are subsequently born. The truth of the Gospel is that Christ is the firstborn of many brethren. Romans 8:29 says, "For whom He did foreknow, He also did predestinate to be conformed to the image of His Son, that He might be the Firstborn among many brethren." He alone, His teachings, His lifestyle are put forth by the Holy Spirit as our only acceptable pattern for learning how to be children of God. 1 Peter 2:21 says, "For even hereunto were ye called: because

Christ also suffered for us, leaving us an example, that ye should follow His steps." We are to grow up into the fullness of the stature of Christ (Eph. 4:13). The Apostle Paul said, "Be ye followers of me, even as I also am of Christ" (1 Cor. 11:1). Christ will not lead you into bondage. He is leading you into greater intimacy with the Father.

Sibling rivalry is an open door for the enemy. When I, as the more seasoned believer, am threatened by the arrival of the new believer, I am open to being used by the enemy to communicate misinformation. Some of you can relate to this simply by remembering tricks that were played on you by older siblings. You may remember things that you were encouraged to do that the encourager knew would get you into trouble. I refer you to the story of the young and the old prophet (Please read this story in 1 Kings 13:1-32, if you are not familiar with it, before you continue reading).

The old prophet maliciously and intentionally used his longer standing in the office of the prophet to instigate disobedience in the younger prophet. Verse 18 says, "He said unto him, I am a prophet also as thou art; and an angel spake unto me by the word of the Lord, saying, Bring him back with thee into thine house, that he may eat bread and drink water. But he lied unto him." Not only did the disobedience cost the young prophet his life, but also his experience is recorded to illustrate to us that in the end we are held responsible for what God has communicated directly to us (*our own hearing*).

It is imperative to your spiritual life that you both hear and know the voice of the Good Shepherd for yourself. John 10: 2-5 says, "But he that entereth in by the door is the shepherd of the sheep. To him the porter openeth; and the sheep hear his voice and he calleth his own sheep by name, and leadeth them out. And when he putteth forth his own sheep, he goeth before them, and the sheep follow him; for they know his voice." At a time when the new born again believer should be establishing his/her ability to hear and obey the voice of the Good Shepherd, the seducing voice of Jezebel can often appear to be louder.

The voice of the Holy Spirit should be valued in much the same way as the voice of E. F. Hutton in their old commercials. The room is full of people. When people in the room realize that E. F. Hutton is about to speak to someone in the room, everyone immediately gets quiet. You could hear a pin drop. No one utters a sound, and all attention is focused on what he is about to speak. This is a good picture of the reverence the voice of the Holy Spirit should have in our lives. When HE speaks, every other voice must be silent. Jesus said, "You have heard that it was said by them of old time.... But I say unto you..." (Matt. 5:21-22). You must hear Him for yourself, even in the voice of others. There should be a distinction between hearing the voice of God in our leaders and letting the voice of our leaders become God. Examine your life, your principles and why you do what you do. What do you follow because of your understanding, and how much of what you do is based on what others have told you?

As children growing up, how many times did we challenge the right of others to control, chastise or discipline us? Instinctively, we either thought or said, "You are not my mother; I don't have to listen to you," questioning their right to interact with us in a specific way. We had to learn as we were growing up that they had received their authority to discipline us from our parents in our parent's absence. The point is that it is in our God-given nature to *question* their authority. When I was growing up in north Philadelphia, every person three years or more my senior could discipline me. And there was more discipline awaiting me when I arrived home if someone had to speak to me outside of the home. Today, it is very difficult to find communities where the disciplining of one another's children is still an acceptable practice. The important thing to note here is that we took our clue from our parents. If they indicated that the person administering the discipline was operating with their blessing, we had no choice but to submit. I believe that same governing attitude should be present in our spiritual lives. The abiding presence of the Holy Spirit should bear witness that what we are receiving from others has the blessing of our Daddy.

When a word of correction, rebuke or exhortation is spoken into our lives, it should line up with the Word of God. It should produce peaceable fruit, even in the presence of a need to repent. Therefore, even in the spirit, we should by nature at least *question* any tendency to be controlled by any spirit or person other than God. Does this mean that we do not respect or appreciate the people God uses? OF COURSE NOT! 1 Thessalonians 5:12–13 says, "And we beseech you, brethren, to know them which labor among you, and are over you in the Lord, and admonish you; and to esteem them very highly in love for their work sake. And be at peace among yourselves." In light of this verse, we may conclude that when we are rightly connected to leadership we will both have and be at peace. There are lines or boundaries separating what is acceptable and what is not acceptable for all of our relationships. Here are just a few examples:

- "Honour thy father and mother" (Matt. 15:4).

- "Therefore as the Church is subject unto Christ, so let the wives be to their own husbands in everything" (Eph. 5:24).

- "Husbands, love your wives, even as Christ also loved the Church, and gave himself for it" (Eph. 5:25).

- "Be kindly affectioned one to another with brotherly love: in honor preferring one another" (Rom. 12:10).

- "Therefore if thou bring thy gift to the altar, and there rememberest that thy brother hath ought against thee; Leave thy gift before the altar, and go thy way; first be reconciled to thy brother, and then come and offer thy gift" (Matt. 5:23-24).

- "But I say unto you, Love your enemies, bless them that curse you, do good to them that hate you, and pray for them which despitefully use you, and persecute you; that ye may be the children of your Father which is in heaven..." (Matt. 5:44-45).

- "Be not forgetful to entertain strangers: for thereby some have entertained angels unawares" (Heb. 13:2).

- "Thou shalt love thy neighbor as thyself" (Gal. 5:14).

From Genesis to Revelations, from Cain and Abel to the brother overtaken in a fault, the Holy Spirit reveals to us the heart of God for ALL of our relationships. If we do not acknowledge that these lines exist, we become vulnerable to being victimized by spirits of control, manipulation, legalism, tradition, religion and witchcraft. As we grow into the fullness of the stature of Christ, we will need to know and respect where these lines are. Ephesians 4:13 says, "Till we all come in the unity of the faith, and of the knowledge of the Son of God, unto a perfect man, unto the measure of the fulness of Christ." Why is it that only in the Body of Christ do we give people free reign? You cannot interact with me in any way that you choose. It is my choice to have all of my relationships rightly formed, according to God's Word and purpose. God is a God of law and order!

Here we have the crux of the matter. Where is the ability of the believer to discern where Christ ends and human nature begins? In order to be free from spiritual witchcraft, we must retain our God-given ability to sense and know when something or someone has veered off into a tangent or spirit of error. 1 John 4:1 (Amplified) says, "Beloved do not put faith in every spirit, but prove (test) the spirits to discover whether they proceed from God; for many false prophets have gone forth into the world."

Without any disrespect, we must be allowed to *question* the voice of God in our leaders. The ever-growing presence of fear perpetuates the diminishing presence of this skill. There is definitely something wrong if you are fearful of asking God to confirm other people's counsel to you. I fully believe that God is raising up an army of believers who are bold enough to say, "I don't receive what you are saying," or, "That does not bear witness with my spirit," not because we are reckless or in rebellion, but because we are serious about being owned and used by God and not by man.

Let me share another example of how we can be under the controlling influence of Jezebel through older siblings. I raised my daughters as a single parent. This required my oldest daughter to take on many responsibilities, and she did a great job with her two younger sisters. Even to this day, what she says to them outweighs most of what I say. Often, I would be talking to one of them and they would say, "But, Teresa said..." which in their minds meant end of discussion. Even though I was the mom, Teresa had been the one cooking for them and watching them after school.

So, when it came time for advice or counsel, they preferred to take it from her, their peer. A statement like "God, I know what you are saying but my prayer partner said..." can be the result of subtle peer pressure. Ultimately, each of us must examine any hesitancy to obey God for the true source of this delay. Are we allowing those around us to influence us too much? Is my hesitancy the result of my own unresolved issues or the issues others have brought into my life?

Needing To Be Accepted

The excitement generated by being a part of something bigger than you can be intoxicating. During what I would call the "glory years" of the movement to which I belonged, we also had several conventions every year. Every three months, we would have *quarterly* meetings. This was a time set aside for the *ruling elder* to come to the local church for an update on the condition of the church. At this meeting, all members were required to be present and to pay a designated amount of money to the elder. The further up a person was in the leadership hierarchy, the more money they were required to pay. Then, there were also three annual conventions, all requiring the payment of money (*reports*).

The entire atmosphere at these conventions was one of competition, ranging from who paid the most money to who could preach the best sermon. It's hard to explain, but sometimes when you are in the momentum of a thing, it can be difficult to <u>see</u> the error in what you are participating. The *truth* is that, once I had been born again into this particular church family, I did many things to be accepted. I didn't know about low self-esteem or the neediness that being abused as a child produces in your adult life.

More truth: I didn't know I had so many issues that needed God's dealing. It was only after I got out of that organization altogether that the floodgate opened. God began to speak to my heart about me. He began to show me areas where I needed healing. Most importantly, I learned to rest in the strength of what I had with Him as opposed to what I had with organized religion.

It is a natural desire to want to please and be accepted. Needing to be validated, to learn self worth and to have parental approval are God-given motivators. They help to push us towards a higher level of obedience. God the Father gave His approval of Jesus at His baptism. "This is my Beloved Son, in Whom I am well pleased; hear ye Him" (Matt. 17:5). As members of the Body of Christ, we must follow the example set forth by God. Members of the Body who are connected directly to God will innately look to Him for approval. Looking to men for recognition, titles and position to establish our worth in the Body of Christ is a learned behavior. I don't see myself as valuable because some people call me "Pastor." I see myself as valuable because Christ paid for me by dying on the Cross. That says to me that I am of value to Him.

Let's go back for a minute to our analogy of the newborn baby. A newborn raised in a nurturing, affirming environment instinctively looks to its parents for approval and acceptance. When I tell my grandbaby, "Good job," she squeals with delight and tries even harder to accomplish whatever task she has undertaken. Therefore, we may make an observation here: If believers are looking to leadership to affirm them, they are not rightly connected. It is appropriate to expect God to use leaders to affirm us. God uses people. The challenge, though, is to be so connected to God that you don't _need_ people to affirm you. I would love for people to be able to see and recognize the call of God on my life. However, I do not need them to recognize my call. I know I am called. I have invested time in His presence to allow Him to convince me of my call. And yes, the confirmation through leadership has come as an added strength to my conviction.

Ephesians 1:6 says, "To the praise of the glory of His grace, wherein He has made us accepted in the Beloved." In order to be productive in the Body of Christ and for the glory of God, we must have the assurance of knowing we are already accepted. Acceptance by God is not to be held out to believers as a golden carrot to be reached for or earned. He makes a distinction between working for Him and being accepted by Him. God has promised to reward our work for Him, our work being tried in the fire (1 Cor. 3:12-15).

> *Now if any man build upon this foundation gold, silver, precious stones, wood, hay, stubble; every man's work shall be made manifest: for the day shall declare it, because it shall be revealed by fire; and the fire shall try every man's work of what sort it is. If any man's work abide which he hath built thereupon, he shall receive a reward. If any man's work shall be burned, he shall suffer loss: but he himself shall be saved; yet so as by fire.*

To equate any type of service in a local church with being accepted in the Body of Christ is wrong. This was absolutely not the message put forth by my church. Not only did you have to do ministry as they dictated, but anyone who did not adhere to the rules that we followed was definitely on their way to hell. For any person, denomination or organization to communicate to any believer that there is only acceptance through them or their belief system is to negate what Christ has done for us. It was His Blood sacrifice alone that has reconciled us to God. Hebrews

10:12 says, "But this Man, after He had offered one sacrifice for sins for ever, sat down on the right hand of God." At the very heart of reconciliation is acceptance. God is not up in heaven trying to decide if He should let me in. When I accepted Christ as my Savior, I got in.

When a baby is born into a family, the family does not take a poll to see if the baby measures up. He or she is a part of the family, period. You have been born into the family of God. God will raise you up without the approval of others. As the baby grows up, he or she might bring honor or dishonor to the family. The family's response to that will vary according to culture and social practices. The Word of God is full of His response to sons that bring both honor and dishonor. Search the Scriptures (John 5:39); know for yourself how to be a son that brings honor (Selah).

We must make a distinction between belonging to a local assembly (a church) and being a part of the Body of Christ (the Church). This seems to be a problem especially here in America. As I travel, I often hear statements about the Body of Christ that only reflect things that are happening in America. America is not the Body of Christ. The Body of Christ is global, and you are a member of that Body already, "accepted in the Beloved" (Eph. 1:6).

I heard it put another way during my last trip to Nigeria. A pastor said to me, "America is so arrogant to have two teams from America playing baseball against each other and call it the World Series." He went on to say that the same arrogance could be seen in the Church in America. 2 Corinthians 10:12 says, "For we dare not make ourselves of the number, or compare ourselves with some that commend themselves: but they measuring themselves by themselves, and comparing themselves among themselves, are not wise." I cannot afford to compare myself to anyone else. I can only accurately assess myself by comparing myself to God's purpose for my life. Therefore, at all cost I must know His purpose and pursue His will.

The Holy Spirit is at work to restore right relationships. We need leadership. We need the five-fold ministry gifts that have been given to the Body of Christ "And He gave some, apostles; and some, prophets; and some, evangelists; and some, pastors and teachers; for the perfecting of the saints, for the work of the ministry, for the edifying of the Body of Christ" (Eph. 4:11-12). Our need to please and be accepted is a part of how

He has made us and is designed to connect us to Him. Once that connection has been established, we should not allow anyone to influence us to disobedience. This is a call to examine our relationships in the light of God's Word, allowing the Holy Spirit to reveal to us the things that are hidden.

Landmark: Have you been influenced to disobedience by anyone in your inner circle? How much weight do you give to the advice and counsel of friends or family? When confronted with a difference of opinion on how to proceed with some aspect of your spiritual life, do you find yourself acquiescing even when it is not what you really believe you should do? Answering YES to any or all of these questions should make you question WHY? What is the influence to which you are submitting, and do you need to get out from under it? Do you have any relationships in your life that you are fearful of losing? Is your sense of acceptance with God tied to how you serve in your local church? Do you feel accepted by God only through good works? How do you know that God accepts you? Is any part of your security in the knowledge of that acceptance dependent on any other relationship? You, with the help of the

Holy Spirit, are the only one who can answer these questions.

Barriers: Not knowing according to Scripture who you are in Christ. Comparing yourself to others. Not knowing the voice of the Good Shepherd for yourself. Insecurity and past hurts rooted in rejection.

Solution: Confess your true feelings, acknowledging areas of past hurts. Do not try to hide or justify How you feel. I have found writing to be very therapeutic. Take out a blank sheet of paper. From memory, write down all of the things that you know God has said about you. Include Scriptures, prophetic words or anything that God has used to reveal to you who you are. After you've written as many as you can remember, compare your list with any written prophecies, etc., you might have. Review your list to see how it compares to Scripture, making a note of what things you know by the Spirit of God and what things you know because people said them. Think about or make a note of anything you wrote that was not based on Scripture. Search the Scriptures for anything you left out, including areas in which you know that your faith needs to be built up.

Prayer: Dear Jesus, I thank You for dying on the Cross for me. I thank You, Lord, that I am accepted in the Beloved. Thank You for Your promise to never leave me or forsake me. I thank You for always being present to help me. I thank You, Lord, for the Body of Christ. Father, I confess to You that I do not always feel loved or wanted. I ask You to forgive me for allowing negative words and thoughts to enslave me. Holy Spirit, lead me to Scriptures that will affirm and establish me in love. Lord, I desire to be rooted and grounded in the knowledge of Your love for me. Open up my understanding even more that I might be able to receive revelation knowledge from You. Let the truth of Your Word come alive in my heart, bringing about change in my everyday life, in Jesus' Name, Amen.

Scripture Helps: Jeremiah 29; Matthew 28; John 6; 2 Corinthians 1; Acts 2; Romans 8; Galatians 6; Ephesians 1.

Chapter Four

Victim Thinking and Denial

Victim Thinking

I have thought about all of these different scenarios at various times over the past 10 years. Writing all this down in one place, over this last year, has made me ask myself a question: "What were you thinking back then?" I can honestly say I wasn't thinking at all. I was letting everyone else think for me, which is another by-product of victim mentality. I had, and still have, a sharp intellectual mind, but when it came to people, I didn't have a clue. I was naïve, innocent, desperate for love and acceptance. I thought everyone was my friend, and honestly didn't know that church folks can lie. Sometimes it is hard for me to speak about those years, but even though things were hard I still don't have any regrets. I believe that everything I experienced was to bring me to this point in purpose and destiny. I am thankful to be able to put into words things that did happen, in order that others might be free. That is the only purpose for this look into my past.

There is a saying: "We are what we eat." The Word of God says that we are what we think. "As a man thinketh in his heart, so he is" (Prov. 23:7). "Death and life are in the power of the tongue: and they that love it shall eat the fruit thereof" (Prov. 18:21); "...that we will have whatsoever we say" (Mark 11:23); and, "O generation of vipers, how can ye, being evil, speak good things? For out of the abundance of the heart, the mouth speaketh" (Matt. 12:34). Therefore, how we think becomes very important, as well as what we say.

The Word of God is the only thing that can change our mind-sets or *how* we think. Romans 12:2 says, "And be not conformed to this world: but be ye transformed by the renewing of your mind..." If you have been under the influence of spiritual witchcraft, you are a victim. Spiritual witchcraft victims subtly and subconsciously are held by how they think, as well as what they think. *Victim mentality thinking* lies deep in the spirit, mind and heart of the victim. To effectively dismantle the stronghold of the enemy, we will examine some common thoughts of victims.

#1 Self-blame. "I provoked the abuse." This is a type of self-loathing. Victims often blame themselves for all types of things.

Recently, I was listening to a teenager in a counseling session. This girl once loved God, and was very much on fire for the Lord. She was a gifted and anointed worship team member. When I met her, she had become very disenchanted with God. After much patience on my part, she began to open up to me and to share her heart. There was such anger and hostility present for someone so young, that I was very concerned for her state of mind.

As she began to tell me her story, my heart broke into tiny little pieces, and I had to pray to keep my own anger in check. In most ways, her story was common to that of many teenage girls and boys. It was a story of repeated sexual abuse by a family member – in this case, her father. However, what sent me to that thin line between anger and sinning was what she shared next. When the truth of this situation came out into the open, she was blamed for the disruption of the family home life. She had received the courage to finally tell her mother.

Naturally, the mother responded by having the father removed from the home. Other things occurred that I won't go into here, but what she said next astounded me. Her father looked her in the face and told her that, had she kept her mouth shut and just dealt with the situation, he would not have lost his job and his family. At the tender age of 13, she had lost her innocence, the love of her siblings (who also blamed her for their daddy having to leave), and her expectation of God being present to protect her. It took time and the wisdom of the Holy Ghost, but eventually I was able to help her see that it was indeed her father who was accountable for his own actions.

Getting over spiritual witchcraft requires the victim to receive a grace that will allow them to hold people accountable for their actions and their words. Silence is a tool that the spirit of Jezebel wields effectively. Victims, through the keeping of secrets, often protect Jezebel. Many suffer silently because of false loyalty.

I remember one such occasion when the spirit of witchcraft was looking for an entrance into my life. I was very young in the ministry. I did not have a clue about hidden motives. I was just skipping along having a wonderful life, when a woman who was later identified as a lesbian attached herself to me. She was a "minister" of the Gospel. She invited me to Indiana to do some meetings. She instructed me to not tell my spiritual mentor. I can't remember now the reason she gave, but I agreed.

Just before I was to leave, I received a phone call from my mentor, asking me what I was about to do. Our relationship was especially graced with honesty that often astounded her. Without thinking about my promise of secrecy, I spilled the beans. Well, you can imagine her response as the Holy Spirit revealed the true intent of my hostess. Needless to say, I didn't go, and I learned a vital lesson for spiritual preservation. I established for myself the standard of: *If I can't tell it, I shouldn't do it.* Glory to God!

#2 Low Self-esteem. Rather than appropriately holding people accountable for their actions, victims often believe that whatever is being done to them is deserved.

The human mind is an awesome reflection of the creative sovereignty of God, "for I am fearfully and wonderfully made: marvelous are Thy works;

and that my soul knoweth right well" (Ps. 139:14). No matter how we try, there remains far more that we don't understand or can't explain than what we do actually understand. For most victims, the only way the mind can accept the abuse is to determine that they deserve the abuse. What other people do to them impacts how they value their own worth. To esteem someone or something is to assess its value. To have low self-esteem means to not give the proper value or to assess a low value to your own worth. To allow the abuse to continue is to place a higher value on the abuser than you do on yourself.

Spiritual witchcraft victims value the voice of others, the counsel of others, above their own ability to hear the voice of the Holy Spirit. Often, the spirit of Jezebel operates through those who have *been saved longer*. I don't deserve to be controlled or manipulated by anyone. Jesus is the one who paid for the right to lead me in the way that I should go. I will place the proper value on myself by properly valuing and guarding His right to lead me. We are instructed to not think of ourselves more highly than we ought. "For I say, through the grace given unto me, to every man that is among you, not to think of himself more highly than he ought to think; but to think soberly, according as God hath dealt to every man the measure of faith" (Rom. 12:3).

We must allow the Holy Spirit to teach us who we are in God. When we know and embrace who we have been created to be, we will challenge any attempt to alter us. I do not have to esteem you lower in order to esteem myself properly. On the contrary, through esteeming myself properly I will also esteem you in the light of His glorious grace. The Apostle Paul said, "For who maketh thee to differ from another? And what hast thou that thou didst not receive? Now if thou didst receive it, why dost thou glory, as if thou hadst not received it?" (1 Cor. 4:7). Who we are, is who He has made us to be, and what we have, we all alike have received. There is no room for boasting or for low self-esteem. *Purpose to be the person God has made you to be.*

#3 Misplaced Trust. "Since I have already deemed you worthy of my trust, when there is abuse, there must be something wrong or missing on my part."

Victim thinking rarely allows the victim to contemplate the idea that maybe the abuser is not trustworthy. In most cases, *victim thinking* centers on one's insufficiencies, hang-ups or

67

shortcomings. This is a by-product of low self-esteem. "You are worthy of my trust." When there is betrayal of that trust, *victim thinking* dictates that there must be something wrong with me. Instead of realizing or accepting that you have been betrayed, you will bear all of the responsibility for being victimized.

Misplaced trust is fueled by the need of the controller to exercise authority. Instead of facilitating an environment where God is the object of our trust, the controller becomes the center of attention. The Psalms are filled with declarations of the trustworthiness of our God. At the heart of our trust in God is the personal revelation of His infallibility. He never fails. He backs His Word and with Him there is no shadow of turning. "Every good gift and every perfect gift is from above, and cometh down from the Father lights, with Whom is no variableness, neither shadow of turning" (James 1:17).

None of us can make such a claim. With all of our good intentions and maturity in Christ, we are still susceptible to missing the mark. In this season in my life, God has given me spiritual sons. It is an awesome privilege and a solemn responsibility. At crucial times in my communications with them, I remind them to look to Jesus. To remember that I am just as they are, perhaps a little further down the road, but no less human and no more divine. They must trust God, and it is my responsibility to constantly shift their focus back to Him, thereby maintaining His pre-eminence in their lives.

#4 Misplaced Loyalty. "I remain loyal to the abuser at the expense of being disloyal to God and myself." This is more clearly seen in children who are abused by their parents.

The tendency for the child to protect rather than betray a parent presents an overwhelming barrier. Usually, intervention from someone outside of the home is necessary to assist a child in revealing any abusive behavior. If controlling, manipulative people are abusing me and I close my eyes to the situation, I am in denial. I also become an enabler. I am sending a message to the abuser that it is OK for him or her to have this type of impact on my life. This is in direct contradiction to what God desires for me. God's desire is to have ownership of a vessel fit for His use, design and purposes.

Spiritual witchcraft victims are fiercely loyal. I have a very dear friend and colleague in Philadelphia. When I first met her she was faithfully serving under the leadership of a known homosexual. For years the Lord had been revealing to her his true condition; you know, the kind of red flags it is easier to ignore than confront. I had never met this man or even heard of him or his church. When, by unction of the Holy Spirit, I began to share with her God's concern for his soul, she became quite defensive.

For some time after that, each of our encounters would be filled with the kind of tension you could cut with a knife. I had spoken more truth than she was ready to admit. After some very painful circumstances converged on their relationship, she was literally forced out by the Holy Spirit. As she began her own journey to freedom, she later confided in me how accurate my statements had proven to be. Her loyalty to him had replaced or blocked a greater loyalty to God. There is no doubt that she has always had a deep abiding love for the Lord, but during that season in her life, her loyalty had been greatly misplaced. Praise God, today she is enjoying complete victory from the spirit of Jezebel.

Denial

Offering excuses for why and how people mistreat us is to be in denial. My love for a person does not diminish when I admit that I have been hurt or betrayed by that person. However, if I am to be free, I must come face to face with my pain. I must be able to say I am hurting. As we examine the life of spiritual witchcraft victims, we are able to see the charade of positive confessions for what it really is.

All too often, believers are hiding their true state of being behind masks or poker faces as the result of being in denial. There are so many wounded believers in the Body of Christ who remain unhealed because of their inability to say, "I am hurt." In order to be free, we must change how we think. Somewhere in our hearts or spirits, we have accepted the thought that we are to be victimized. Thinking or reasoning that allows us to accept victimization must be brought into captivity by the truth of God's Word.

God did not send His Son to set you free for you to be victimized or brought into bondage by other believers. ("If the Son therefore shall make you free, ye shall be free indeed," John 8:36.) To be controlled, to be manipulated or to be intimidated by others is wrong. It is _wrong_! Let that sink in. No one has the right to control you, and to _think_ otherwise is to embrace spiritual death. Jesus came that, "you might have life, and have it more abundantly (John 10:10)." Within that abundant life is liberty. God desires for you to be free in every area of your life. If you are going to be free from spiritual witchcraft, you must choose to come out of denial. You must choose to stop thinking as a victim and to embrace the thoughts and the Word of God concerning your freedom. You must be first partaker in embracing who you are in the Body, what has been given to you and what God expects from you. To live in the freedom of whom God has made you is to embrace His thoughts, His purpose and His plan as the only guide for your life.

People who are victimized share the common bond of vulnerability. In order for someone to victimize us, we must be made vulnerable. By brute force, the presence of a weapon, our own fears or cunning maneuvers, the person victimizing us must be stronger in some way. *Getting out* from under the influence of spiritual witchcraft requires an understanding and an acceptance of the fact that we are no longer vulnerable. Romans 8:31 says, "What shall we say then to these things? If God be for us, who can be against us?" There is no longer any need to think like a victim. "The Spirit itself (Himself) beareth witness with our spirit, that we are the children of God: and if children, then heirs; heirs of God and joint-heirs with Christ; if so be that we suffer with him, that we may be also glorified together" (Rom. 8:16-17). We are not left to our own devices. We do not have to fight for ourselves. God is on our side. Believing that, and knowing that, will produce corresponding actions. We are no longer victims.

Landmark: Who continues to treat you as a victim when God has set you free? Are you still thinking like a victim? In your own mind and heart, do you still see yourself as weak and helpless? What do you need to do to stop treating yourself like a victim? Have you opened yourself up to spiritual witchcraft through self-pity? Are you reluctant to face the truth about the motives of those with whom you interact? Do you know those that labor with you?

Barriers: Not allowing your gift of discernment to have free course. Attempting to protect yourself from heartache by denying the truth. Not knowing the voice of the Holy Spirit.

Solution: Come out of denial and make a commitment to know the truth. God has given us our feelings. Allow yourself to feel. Jesus is touched with the feeling of our infirmities. When you express to Him how you feel, He is touched. You have His attention, and He ever makes intercession for you. He will fight for you. Build your self-esteem through studying the Word of God. Search out teachings on your righteousness. Meditate on the Word. And maybe most importantly be willing to invest in yourself.

Prayer: Lord, I confess to You that I am hurting. I have feelings that I don't understand and some I don't even like. I lay it all at Your feet. I ask You to heal me from the inside out. Lord, pour out Your spirit and close every open wound. Help me to deal honestly with any unresolved issues. Bring closure to every situation that is behind me. Father, I thank You that I am a new creation in You. Old things are passed away and all things are new. I thank You for discernment. Open my eyes that I might see, and my ears that I might hear. Speak to my heart. Lord, I want to hear and know Your voice. Father, I ask that the Holy Spirit will continue to work in my life and in my heart, that I might receive the mind of Christ, in Jesus' Name, Amen.

Scripture Helps: Isaiah 26; Proverbs 23; Acts 17; Romans 7, 12; Philippians 2; 2 Thessalonians 2; Hebrews 8; 1 Peter 1, 4.

Chapter Five

Fear and Intimidation

Fear

I was doing well, or so I thought. I was moving on up in the big league. I had favor with the bishops, one in particular who had propositioned me. I was paying all of my reports. I faithfully attended every service, convention, etc. I went through all of the licensing procedures. I studied to show myself approved, and I was rewarded.

The use of fear and intimidation in this particular denomination was nothing less than masterful. In the name of reverence, we all bowed to a bishop we knew to have more than one mistress. In public or private, we would never call a leader by their first name for fear that lightening would strike us dead. To disagree with one of the leaders was to be publicly reprimanded with the appropriate amount of humiliation. This standard of respect and being sexually abused produced a perverted fear of God in me. I pictured Him standing up in heaven with a big club. Anytime I did anything wrong, I thought He was waiting there to crack me over the head. When I look back, it amazes me to think that I actually believed that I was free. The *truth* is that I was bound by all types of fear and held hostage by the spirit of Religion.

I was in a comfort zone. I knew the rules. I knew how to succeed in my environment. I knew how to maneuver and do some manipulating of my own. It was quite an undertaking for me to reconcile with the idea that God wanted me out. Looming very heavily over me was fear of failure and fear of backsliding. I had been submitting to authority that taught me that to be separated from them was synonymous with being separated from God. I have been in charismatic circles where it has been taught that, "if you leave here, you won't be blessed." The believer who is rightly connected to God must be allowed to take risks. If I believe I am obeying a directive from God, you must release me in love. If I have missed God, HE knows how to bring me back on course. Relationships that are void of manipulation are easy to maintain and also void of the fear of loss because of disapproval.

Fear is a breeding ground and open door to the enemy. Paul says, "God has not given us the spirit of fear, but of power and of love and of a sound mind" (2 Tim. 1:7). I don't know of anything more crippling than fear. Fear can and will literally paralyze its victim. As I was beginning to write this chapter, I reached for the dictionary. I love word studies, and I love the dictionary. As I began to read the definition of synonyms for the word fear, I realized that to include the actual meanings would bring some added clarity. So, please take your time and let the words sink in. I promise you, we are going somewhere powerful in our quest to be free.

- **Fear** – a feeling of agitation and anxiety caused by present or imminent danger.

- **Fright** – sudden, usually momentary, great fear.

- **Dread** – strong fear, especially of what one is powerless to avoid.

- **Terror** – intense overpowering fear.

- **Horror –** a combination of fear and aversion and/or repugnance.

- **Panic –** sudden frantic fear, often groundless.

- **Alarm –** fright aroused by the first realization of danger.

- **Dismay –** robs one of courage or the power to act effectively.

- **Consternation –** often paralyzing, characterized by confusion and helplessness.

- **Trepidation –** a dread, characteristically marked by trembling or hesitancy.

In elementary school, when we would receive a new list of spelling words, we would be required to write them three times and use the word in a sentence to demonstrate that we understood what the word meant. Here is one for the good old days. "_Fear_ produced _fright,_ leading to feelings of _dread, terror,_ and _horror_ that caused me to _panic_ and be spun into _alarm. Dismayed_ by my dilemma, _consternation_ settled in and _trepidation_ has held me captive."

When I was raising my daughters, we used to have these little scenes at the dinner table. I have one daughter who was afraid to try anything new. She would look at the food, and if there was something new or something cooked differently, her immediate response would be, "I don't like that." Now mind you, she never tasted it. At least then, I could have forced myself to respect her taste. But for her to declare that she didn't like it before she tasted it would invariably send her sisters into a lengthy commentary. After so many repeat episodes, we eventually stopped offering her what was *new and different.*

How sad it is to know that there are members in the Body of Christ who consistently reject *new and different,* mostly motivated by fear. Fear of change; fear of rejection and fear of the unknown hold us hostage, enslaving us to repetitive cycles. Willingness and an ability to take risks will help to release you from the grip of spiritual witchcraft. Fear is not to be confused with reverence or respect. In *Chapter Two,* CHILDLIKE FAITH VS. BLIND FAITH, we discussed "how" we are to respect our leaders. Reverence, "a feeling of profound awe and respect and often, love," is reserved for God alone and not optional. You probably know someone who is afraid of something. There are approximately 530 "phobias and fears." Of what are you afraid? Job said, "The thing which I greatly feared is come upon me, and that which I was afraid of is come unto me" (Job 3:25).

I have one colleague who was afraid to hear anything negative about another colleague. I never did understand how or what this knowledge did to him. When confronted with information of some wrong doing by a leader, he would respond by saying, "To the pure all things are pure." Actually, he was fearful of receiving any knowledge of another person's weakness or shortcoming. He just did not want to know it, so he systematically tried to protect himself by quoting this Scripture. Often, he was left hurt, disappointed and in shock when more serious things would happen with these same individuals.

What things are you holding at bay because of fear? I suppose if it were possible to poll believers at large, we would be astonished to know how many of us have done battle with the "fear of what others will think." This one fear alone could be dubbed "the believer slayer." When you really consider this dilemma, it is mind-boggling.

There is one observation that I would like to offer as an effective antidote for the "fear of man" disease. It is intimacy with the Father, Jesus and the Holy Spirit. Through intimacy, the apostles were able to receive grace that conquered all of their fears. Being led to death as martyrs, they were consistently able to override every fear, fulfilling the mandate upon their lives. I am sure they had their moments. Some of them are recorded for us in Peter's denial and Thomas' doubt. I am not saying that you won't have your moments also. I am saying that I believe there is a place "under the shadow of the Almighty" (Ps. 91:1) that will give to us the victory. Dwelling in the secret place closes the open door of fear.

Intimidation

Where low self-esteem and insecurity are already present, fear and intimidation become a deadly force in the lives of believers. With the animalistic instincts of a dog, when the spirit of Jezebel senses fear in a believer, she launches her attack. When the apostles were commanded not to speak anymore in the Name of Jesus, they responded by asking for more boldness (Acts 4:13-31).

Now when they saw the boldness of Peter and John, and perceived that they were unlearned and ignorant men, they marvelled; and they took knowledge of them, that they had been with Jesus. And beholding the man which was healed standing with them, they could say nothing against it. But when they had commanded them to go aside out of the council, they conferred among themselves, saying, What shall we do to these men? For that indeed a notable miracle hath been done by them is manifest to all them that dwell in Jerusalem; and we cannot deny it. But that it spread no further among the people, let us straitly threaten them, that they speak henceforth to no man in this Name.

And they called them, and commanded them not to speak at all nor teach in the Name of Jesus. But Peter and John answered and said unto them, Whether it be right in the sight of God to hearken unto you more than unto God, judge ye. For we cannot but speak the things which we have seen and heard. So when they had further threatened them, they let them go, finding nothing how they might punish them, because of the people: for all men glorified God for that which was done. For the man was above forty years old, on whom this miracle of healing was showed.

And being let go, they went to their own company, and reported all that the chief priests and elders had said unto them. And when they heard that, they lifted up their voice to God with one accord, and said, Lord, Thou art God, which hast made heaven, and earth, and the sea, and all that in them is: Who by the mouth of Thy servant David hast said, Why did the heathen rage, and the people imagine vain things? The kings of the earth stood up, and the rulers were gathered together against the Lord, and against His Christ. For of a truth against Thy Holy Child Jesus, whom Thou hast anointed, both Herod, and Pontius Pilate, with the Gentiles, and the people of Israel, were gathered together, For to do whatsoever Thy hand and Thy counsel determined before to be done.

And now, Lord, behold their threatenings: and grant unto Thy servants, that with all boldness they may speak Thy Word, By

*stretching forth Thine hand to heal; and
that signs and wonders may be done by
the Name of Thy Holy Child Jesus. And
when they had prayed, the place was
shaken where they were assembled
together; and they were all filled with the
Holy Ghost, and they spake the Word of
God with boldness.*

The religious officials of the day tried to
intimidate them into submission, the ultimate
goal being a desire to silence them. Until this very
day, the enemy seeks to silence us through the
use of intimidation. Intimidation is used in a
unique way in the realm of spiritual witchcraft. It
is put forth in an air of superiority. Often, those
exercising intimidation present themselves as
having "special" revelation or gifting or anointing.

I had joined a charismatic church for the
expressed purpose of receiving more ministry
training. A prerequisite for participating in the
program was a recognizable call to five-fold
ministry (Eph. 4:11-12). I learned some new
things about the ministry, as well as having my
foundation strengthened. However, at the finish of
the program (one year later) it was announced to
the general congregation that none of the people
who participated in the program had a call to five-

fold ministry. This assessment was very damaging. We all were called, as long as we were serving this local congregation. When the time came to release us into further ministry, as promised, we were told we didn't have the gifts or callings we thought we had.

Even after this announcement, I remained and took a position on staff. My belief that God had called me to full time ministry held me there with a false hope. It was several months later while in a staff meeting that a statement was made which compelled me to take action. The leadership said, "What you are doing right now is that to which you are called." This statement was made with the expressed purpose of manipulating us into remaining in service to that local congregation.

Once again Jezebel was speaking forth its agenda. We learn to serve God and how to walk in the call upon our lives by serving others. However, God is the one ordering my steps. I might be assigned to a season of preparation that involves handling my leaders' personal mail. That doesn't mean that is my final destination in the realm of fulfilling my purpose. When the Lord is ordering my steps, then all of my training will be beneficial and is not to be despised.

If you seek to control me, pimping my gifts to build your kingdom during my time of training, then you will be vulnerable to making assessments that are not accurate. No one knows the mind of God. Who can say that what a person is doing right now is what they are called to do permanently. David, Elisha, Peter, Timothy, just to name a few, all served leadership and at the appointed time came into the fullness of what God had for them. The words spoken to intimidate me into submission motivated me to move on.

Intimidation is the "voice" of the bully. The bully is counting on "speaking" enough to hold you in defeat. He is not expecting you to fight back. When Jezebel puts forth its words as prophetic direction or insight, it will take the sword of the Word to defeat her words. While traveling recently, the Lord shared something with me that I found intriguing. He said, "Lynda, when I speak forth a directive to you, you immediately look inward. This produces thoughts like "I can't" or "I am not able" and, most commonly, "How can I do that?" You look to yourself and only see yourself. However, when I am speaking forth instruction or directives, I only see the Blood of my Son. I speak to you based on what I have put in you and in accordance with My purposes for your life." Intimidation always provokes us to look inwardly. Through experience I say to you who are struggling with intimidation, keep looking inward until you see "Christ in you the hope of Glory" (Col. 1:27).

Landmark: Can you identify exactly what you fear? As you reflect on past conversations, can you detect words that were spoken to bind you? Do you succumb to any bullying in any of your relationships? Is your fear of God greater than your fear of man?

Barriers: Not speaking up when confronted by individuals seeking to control you. Not wanting to rock the boat. Not studying the Word of God to dismantle your fears. Being too hard on yourself for having fear. Moving in guilt or condemnation instead of receiving forgiveness for confessed weaknesses or shortcomings.

Solution: To overcome the barrier of fear and intimidation, we must allow the love of God to be perfected in our hearts and in our lives. "Perfect love casts out all fear" (1 John 4:18), including fear of man. To avoid being made vulnerable to witchcraft through the open door of "fear" requires open confession of your fears. As you admit your fears, the Holy Spirit will bring the Word of God that deals with your fear. You will hear, read or see something that addresses what you confess. Make a list of any or all of your fears. Ask the Holy Spirit to lead you to Scriptures that will address each one of your concerns. Through the use of a concordance or by asking a Bible teacher, you can find the Word of God that will address your particular concern. You can disarm the devil with the truth of God's Word.

Prayer: Father, I thank You for power, love and a sound mind. I confess my fears to You and ask You to forgive me. I ask You now to let Your love saturate my being. Fill every empty place with more of Yourself. Show me how to receive more of Your love. Give me sensitivity to You and the things of the Spirit. Lord, give me an appetite for Your Word. Grant me more boldness, and teach me how to walk in the authority that You have given me, in Jesus' Name. Lord, I want to be totally available to You. I choose to not let any other spirit have dominion over me. By Your grace, I cut off every voice that would speak contrary to Your Word. I thank You for building a hedge of protection around me. I know that You have given Your angels charge over me and I receive Your peace, in Jesus' Name, Amen.

Scripture Helps: Genesis 15, 21, 26, 42; Exodus 14; Leviticus 25; Numbers 14; Psalm 23, 27, 37, 61, 90; Proverbs 9; Matthew 8; Luke 12; Acts 4; 1 John 4.

SECTION TWO

"Brethren, I count not myself to have apprehended: but this one thing I do, forgetting those things which are behind, and reaching forth unto those things which are before, I press toward the mark for the prize of the high calling of God in Christ Jesus"

Philippians 3:13-14

Chapter Six

Getting Over

Letting Go of the Past

Realizing that I had been duped produced an anger in me that took time to get over. I was hot. I don't know if I was most angry with my abusers or myself. One thing was certain – I was very angry. For months after I left, I couldn't even go to a church of any kind. I remember very clearly standing in my living room and saying out aloud to God, "I love You... I can't stand Your people." Needless to say, I'm glad that God knows when to respond and what to let just pass over. One good thing that did come out of the upheaval of my spiritual life was an opportunity for the Lord to finally speak to me more directly.

As I stewed in my discontent, there was light at the end of the tunnel that started to seep through to my soul. I had decided to give up religion altogether, and enrolled in barber school. God is so gracious and He allowed this, setting me up as only He can.

At school, my seat assignment was right next to a happy born-again believer. It wasn't long before he started to inquirer about my spiritual condition, as he had discerned immediately that I was a preacher. It took some doing on his part, but after weeks of being harassed, I finally agreed to attend a prayer meeting at his church – a church that just happened to be about 10 blocks from the school we were attending. When I entered the church building that night, I had no real expectations. I thought, "Finally I will get him off my back." What happened next has stayed with me as one of the greatest moments in my spiritual life.

When we arrived, prayer was already in progress. People were kneeling throughout the sanctuary, praying just above a whisper. I found a good place to hide and got down on my knees. As I knelt there, my heart began to melt, and instead of me bombarding God with my list of wants, I could hear a still, small voice speaking directly to my heart. The Lord said, "Tonight I take you all the way back to where you first received salvation. I am removing everything that you were taught, and we will start over. You have allowed religion and the thoughts of men to contaminate you. Tonight I wipe the slate clean, and we start afresh." Needless to say, I cried like a baby. Great peace and a sense of being cleansed or washed literally subdued my soul. For the first time, I realized that what I had spent almost 20 years doing was not what He had in mind or had intended for me at all. Rapidly, pictures, words, circumstances and situations began to flood my mind as the Holy Spirit began to unravel my life, and the healing had begun. Just remembering it now brings such sweetness to me. He knows how to set us free. His timing is always perfect.

Getting over spiritual witchcraft, the pain of betrayal, the shame of having been victimized, requires a conscious decision to release everything and everyone who has had any part in your experience. This "releasing" must take place on many levels and may extend over a period of time. You must choose to bring closure, and allow inner healing.

As we examine Elijah's encounter with Jezebel after the slaying of the prophets of Baal, we can see all of the barriers to getting over an encounter with spiritual witchcraft. Elijah had moved into withdrawal and was operating in doubt and unbelief. He had been intimidated and was fearful because of Jezebel's words that she sent by a messenger. The only way Elijah could get over what he had experienced was to have a personal visitation. 1 Kings 19 speaks of Elijah's request to die as he sat under the Juniper tree. Then, the angel instructed him to eat that he might receive strength.

And Ahab told Jezebel all that Elijah had done, and withal how he had slain all the prophets with the sword. Then Jezebel sent a messenger unto Elijah, saying, So let the gods do to me, and more also, if I make not thy life as the life of one of them by to morrow about this time. And when he saw that, he arose, and went for his life, and came to Beersheba, which belongeth to Judah, and left his servant there. But he himself went a day's journey into the wilderness, and came and sat down under a juniper tree: and he requested for himself that he might die; and said, It is enough; now, O Lord, take away my life; for I am not better than my fathers.

And as he lay and slept under a juniper tree, behold, then an angel touched him,

100

and said unto him, Arise and eat. And he looked, and, behold, there was a cake baken on the coals, and a cruse of water at his head. And he did eat and drink, and laid him down again. And the angel of the Lord came again the second time, and touched him, and said, Arise and eat; because the journey is too great for thee. And he arose, and did eat and drink, and went in the strength of that meat forty days and forty nights unto Horeb the mount of God.

And he came thither unto a cave, and lodged there; and, behold, the word of the Lord came to him, and he said unto him, What doest thou here, Elijah? And he said, I have been very jealous for the Lord God of hosts: for the children of Israel have forsaken Thy covenant, thrown down Thine altars, and slain Thy prophets with the sword; and I, even I only, am left; and they seek my life, to take it away. And he said, Go forth, and stand upon the mount before the Lord.

And, behold, the Lord passed by, and a great and strong wind rent the mountains, and brake in pieces the rocks before the

Lord; but the Lord was not in the wind: and after the wind an earthquake; but the Lord was not in the earthquake: And after the earthquake a fire; but the Lord was not in the fire: and after the fire a still small voice. And it was so, when Elijah heard it, that he wrapped his face in his mantle, and went out, and stood in the entering in of the cave. And, behold, there came a voice unto him, and said, What doest thou here, Elijah? And he said, I have been very jealous for the Lord God of hosts: because the children of Israel have forsaken Thy covenant, thrown down Thine altars, and slain Thy prophets with the sword; and I, even I only, am left; and they seek my life, to take it away.

And the Lord said unto him, Go, return on thy way to the wilderness of Damascus: and when thou comest, anoint Hazael to be king over Syria: And Jehu the son of Nimshi shalt thou anoint to be king over Israel: and Elisha the son of Shaphat of Abelmeholah shalt thou anoint to be prophet in thy room. And it shall come to pass, that him that escapeth the sword of Hazael shall Jehu slay: and him that escapeth from the sword of Jehu shall Elisha slay. Yet I have left me seven thousand in Israel, all the knees which have not bowed unto Baal, and every mouth which hath not kissed him.

In your life, as the victim of spiritual witchcraft, you come to a place in your quest to be free where you have to **get over** what happened to you. Once you are out of the abusive situation, your next step has to be to **get over** it. You must get over it in your mind and in your heart. I realize the difficulty of this from my own personal experience. Letting go of the past is imperative. You cannot change the past. There is nothing you can say or do that will rewrite your history. However, you can change your future.

The difficulty of **getting over** this kind of traumatic experience reminds me of a child who scrapes his or her knee, perhaps from an accidental fall. The crying reinforces the trauma to the child. The mother is trying to get close enough to the wound to administer first aid, which would stop the hurt. The child is in fight mode because the pain is so great – not wanting it touched and at the same time crying to get the pain to stop.

There are many victims of spiritual witchcraft in the Body of Christ who have suffered great trauma to their spirit man. They want the pain to stop, but they do not allow anyone to get close enough to touch the place where they are hurting. The Holy Spirit is uniquely able to touch the place that hurts and to administer the love of God in a healing way. It takes the love of God to really heal us. It's not just reading about the love of God or hearing great sermons about the love of God. It's an ability to allow that love to come in and to touch the place where we were hurting. When I knelt down in that church, I immediately encountered the love of God. He totally enveloped me as He began to speak to my pain.

In order to be free, in order to **get over** what has been done to me in an abusive way, I must let the truth of God's love come in and saturate my very being. How do you accomplish that in your everyday life? By saying, "Yes, I received wrong counsel from leadership, but God loves me. Yes, I might have opened the door to be controlled by being insecure, but God loves me. Yes, what they did to me was wrong, but God loves me." You must meditate on, read about and speak out that love until you both believe and know it. Accepting the love of God for us releases our love for Him.

Our love for God is what motivates us to be obedient. To give God complete ownership of our lives, to make Jesus Lord and Master indeed, we must become saturated with the love of God. Love works obedience in us. Not any promise of heaven or the fear of hell, but the love. "God, I am going to obey You because I love You. I love You."

I can recall another time when I was hurting very badly because of having to let some relationships go. I knew that God was requiring this of me, but that didn't lessen the pain. As I was crying out to the Lord, I began to repeat over and over these words: "Lord, I love You. I love You, Jesus." I began screaming at the top of my lungs. "Lord, do You hear me? I love You." Then, the Holy Spirit whispered something to me that will never leave me. He said, "Lynda, you don't love Me any more than I love you." Profound isn't it, but yet so simple. The pain in my life had caused me to forget just how much I am loved. Regardless of what I must pass through with people, God's love is sufficient. **Getting over** what happens in the area of human relationships diminishes in the remembrance of how much God loves me.

Accept It

IT HAPPENED! The love and peace of God I experienced that night had opened the door for "truth" to get in. The God whom I had learned to fear in an unhealthy manner now had totally disarmed me. He was presenting a side or facet of Himself about which I knew very little, if anything. He was so tender with me, causing me to remember how I had loved Him in the beginning of my spiritual walk with Him. Slowly, skillfully He began to open my eyes to "truth" that needed to be accepted.

In the beginning of becoming free, it is not as important to understand the "truth" that is being presented, as it is to accept what is being presented as the "truth." When the Holy Spirit brings truth to our conscious minds, it will help us to remember that His motives are pure. He has no hidden agenda. His desire is and always has been to draw us closer to Jesus. When we consider the lengths to which God goes, it is easier for us to comprehend just how important His fellowship with us is to Him. At this point in our quest to be free, God requires only one thing from us, a total acceptance of the truth that He is presenting.

106

If we are to move on into the "fullness of the stature of Christ" (Eph. 4:13), we must learn to accept the things that He allows. One of the problems we are confronted with when we are faced with accepting that we have been victimized is the "feeling" that somehow that acceptance excuses the party inflicting the abuse. However, the opposite of acceptance is denial. Hence, this is a call to come out of denial.

How many times have we seen news reports about the murder of some woman who could not or would not leave an abusive relationship? "The thief cometh not, but for to steal, and to kill, and to destroy: I am come that they may have life, and that they might have it more abundantly" (John 10:10). We know in our hearts that those who commit such acts are under the influence of the devil, the thief. Does that negate our observation that the victim should have taken some course of action? No, it does not. In fact, we grieve and empathize that if only she would have accepted the reality of her situation and done something, she might still be alive. I must confess that as someone who has been set free, I am grieved as I am engaged in conversations with believers in abusive churches and abusive spiritual relationships. The question that inevitably arises is, "Why do they stay?"

For most people, the answer is the presence of one or more barriers. Because something is identified as a barrier doesn't make it any less real. To endeavor to be free from the influence of spiritual witchcraft is to engage in a real war. Betrayal, unforgiveness, bitterness and withdrawal are just a few of the barriers that present themselves. The only way to overcome these barriers is to shine the light of God's Word into our thoughts, and to make a conscious decision to let the Word of God have pre-eminence.

The truth of God's Word can dismantle anything that would hinder us from being free. "For the weapons of our warfare are not physical (weapons of flesh and blood), but they are mighty before God for the overthrow and destruction of strongholds; casting down imaginations, and every high thing that exalteth itself against the knowledge of God, and bringing into captivity every thought to the obedience of Christ" (2 Cor. 10:4-5, Amplified).

If you have taken the necessary steps to obey God, you have the grace to **get over** your pain.

It's another type of victory to which you are laying hold. Most often, we think of bondage as being sins of the flesh. Unfortunately, there are many other things that enslave believers. Spiritual witchcraft is something else from which God wants you free. He wants your soul free from any controlling, manipulative influences. He wants us all to come into a place of total surrender to Him. When He speaks forth a directive, He wants our response to be solely based upon our relationship with Him. We are His Bride. No groom wants to have to get permission from someone else to interact with or be with his bride.

Landmark: Can you at this very moment make a conscious decision to get over what has happened to you? Are you fully persuaded that your past is in the past? Can you open your heart to the love of God? Do you really know how much God loves you? How do you measure how much God loves you?

Barriers: Giving too much weight to what people think or what they do to you. Not being able to separate what people do from what God does. Not being able to put out of your mind things that are in the past. Not being able to accept that which has already occurred as over and done.

Solution: You must accept what cannot be changed. Ask the Holy Spirit for wisdom to know how to get over what has happened to you. Sometimes, a good cry or going somewhere to scream at the top of your lungs will bring relief. Do not let yourself be held captive by old mindsets or the past. If you continue to do what you have always done, you will always get the same outcome. Make a resolution to not let anyone or anything hold you hostage, by not being able to get over what you cannot change. Every time a memory assaults your mind, address it with the Word of God. Don't just meditate on the memory. Be aggressive in your fight to move on. Don't make allowances or provision for self-pity.

Prayer: Lord, Your promises to me are "yea and amen." I accept Your provision for abundant life in Christ Jesus. I thank You for Your love, which casts out all fear. Grant me more boldness and the grace that I need to get over my past hurts. Holy Spirit, give me what I need to be able to get over what has happened to me. Lord, let my reverential fear of You supersede my fear of man. Help me, Lord, to guard my heart. Help me to see as You see. Father, if I have allowed any person or organization to replace You on the throne of my heart, forgive me

110

now, in Jesus' Name. My desire is for You. My hope is in You, and my expectation is from You.

Scripture Helps: Genesis 15, 21, 26, 42; Exodus 14; Leviticus 25; Numbers 14; Psalm 23, 27, 61, 90; Isaiah 43; Matthew 8; Luke 12; 2 Timothy 1; 1 John 4.

Chapter Seven

Betrayal, Withdrawal and Isolation

Betrayal

My experience with spiritual witchcraft was not limited to the Holiness church. I have belonged to charismatic churches where the spirit of Jezebel was alive and well. Because spirits of control and manipulation use people, **anywhere** you have a gathering of people you will find these spirits in operation – some places more than others, but no place seems to have a monopoly.

When I came out of the denominational church, I was very wounded. I felt betrayed, and really had no desire to be around "church folks." I did not trust anybody, and had a serious bout with wanting to remain in isolation. One indication that the Lord had truly healed me from the inside was my being able to trust and fellowship once again with the saints. I had to come out of my pity party and let in more truth. Because I was not rightly connected from the beginning, everything that proceeded from my past spiritual relationships was tainted. I did not know how to relate rightly to leadership. I did not know how to respond to controlling people. I had to allow the Holy Spirit to lay a right foundation. I also had to allow Him to be more involved in what was being built upon that foundation. I had to learn to trust Him, His insights and revelations.

Jesus is our example and the Image into which we grow. Let us consider how He handled betrayal. One might be tempted to say that Jesus did not have to interact or deal with Judas after the betrayal, so His experience is different than mine. There is some truth in that observation, but not the entire truth. Where we might find it difficult to forgive and deal with people after they betray us, Jesus had to love, embrace and commune with Judas, knowing that he would betray him. "But there are some of you that believe not. For Jesus knew from the beginning who they were that believed not, and who should betray him" (John 6:64). The question then arises, "How many of us could embrace, love and fellowship, over an extended period of time, with someone we knew would betray us?" This is rarely, if ever, required of us. But Jesus, in so doing, has set the mark of excellence that we may, through and by His grace, forgive and release those who do indeed betray us.

The dictionary defines the act of betrayal: "to give aid or information to an enemy; to deliver into the hands of an enemy in violation of a trust or allegiance; to be false or disloyal; to lead astray, deceive." We can see from these definitions how devastating it is to be betrayed. Spiritual witchcraft very seldom operates through those who are strangers to us. There could be no betrayal without the presence of trust, and an expectation of loyalty. The spirit of Jezebel uses a person that we should be able to trust to turn us over to the enemy. In this case, the enemy is spirits of control and manipulation. We all know what to expect from an enemy, but Jezebel represents itself as a friend, mentor or colleague. Psalm 55:12-14 reads:

"For it was not an enemy that reproached me; then I could have borne it: neither was it he that hated me that did magnify himself against me; then I would have hid myself from him: But it was thou, a man mine equal, my guide, and mine acquaintance. We took sweet counsel together, and walked unto the house of God in company."

We also need to consider how much of our sense of betrayal is actual and how much is the result of wrong expectations. When we are latched onto the breast of Jesus, we will have right and realistic expectations of those with whom we interact. It is wrong to:

1. expect people to save us,

2. expect people to be the voice of god to us,

3. expect people to be perfect,

4. expect our leaders to "hear" for us,

5. expect others to tell us our purpose,

6. expect people to live up to our expectations.

We have very little difficulty remaining in friendships that have been proven. But betrayal brings scars that are both deep and wide. In the end, we must choose to forgive all betrayals, real or perceived. As we release those who have betrayed us, we release ourselves to move on.

Withdrawal and Isolation

It is normal to retreat when we have been wounded. We all have the natural instinct to protect ourselves from further injury by withdrawing. Taking time to ourselves for healing is good and necessary. However, a prolonged period of isolation is dangerous "because your adversary the devil, as a roaring lion, walketh about, seeking whom he may devour" (1 Pet. 5:8). Isolation from the Body of Christ becomes a strategic, effective tool of the enemy. We are referred to in Scripture as sheep. The sheep that has left the fold is the one that is preyed upon by a wolf. We must not give in to the temptation to stay at home, cutting off an entire assembly of believers because of the deeds of a few. Doing that would be allowing one past experience to have an eternal impact. Who can afford that? But when there has been forgiveness from the heart, we will allow our wounds to be healed. With the direction of the Holy Spirit, we can be restored to fellowship, enjoying and receiving all the blessings that flow forth from corporate worship.

It would be appropriate to acknowledge here that there are wonderful churches with faithful, loving leadership. This is not a call to abandon the Body of Christ or a cover for those who are in rebellion against spiritual authority. It is a call to wholeness and healing. We are a Body of believers. The Apostle Paul teaches "that every joint supplies" (Eph. 4:16). Therefore, if you withdraw your presence from the body, you create a void. We are lacking something that God intended us to have. You are not here or in the Body of Christ by accident. You have been brought into the kingdom for such a time as this. We need you. We need the gifts and hidden treasure that is locked up inside of you. You are unique, and no one else can bring to the body what you have been designed to bring.

Think about this. You have a hand as a part of your body. Do you expect your hand to carry out all of the things necessary for you to function in life? No. So it is in the spirit. No one ministry gift or group of ministry gifts can carry out everything that is necessary for the Church to function in this world. We need every member that Christ has set in the Church. We need you to get over what has happened to you.

Landmark: What do you need to do or have happen to be able to put your experience in the past? How much time are you willing to waste while you stew over something that cannot be changed? How valuable is the call of God upon your life to you? What is most important to you: going on with God or being vindicated?

Barriers: Not being able to separate people from the demonic forces that might use them. Misidentifying a person or organization as your enemy. Not giving the proper value to your function in the body at large. Not being able to see the bigger picture. Not recognizing the presence of oppressive spirits. Being unaware of being in a depressed state of mind.

Solution: Ask the Holy Spirit to lead you to a fellowship where you will be accepted. Forgive anyone who has betrayed your trust. Make sure that you are holding the right individuals accountable for their actions, words and deeds. Forgive yourself for allowing open doors to the enemy.

Prayer: Father, I thank You that You are in control of my life. You order my steps, and You lead me in the way that I should go. Lord, You are the only One Who can place me where I belong in the Body of Christ. If I have submitted to any spirit other than the Holy Spirit, please forgive me in Jesus' Name. Holy Spirit, help me to know my purpose, and bring divine connections that will help me to fulfill my purpose in the earth. Holy Spirit, help me to be led not by my feelings, but to be led by You. Give me a greater sensitivity to Your seasons and timings in Jesus' Name. Lord, as I go through this process, heal my wounded spirit and restore me to fellowship with the saints. Lord, turn to good what the enemy has meant for harm as I put my trust in You. I give You all the praise; the glory and the honor belong to You. In Jesus' Name, I pray, Amen.

Scripture Helps: Psalm 22, 35, 89, 107, 111, 149; Matthew 7; Acts 2; Romans 12; 1 Sorinthians 1; Ephesians 4; Philippians 3; Hebrews 10; 1 Peter 5; 1 John 1.

Chapter Eight

Doubt and Unbelief

Doubt

Another by-product of my experience in the denominational church was the presence of doubt and unbelief. When I got saved in 1969, I enjoyed the kind of boldness that comes from being new to the faith. You probably can also remember the kind of faith you had when you first got saved. Mountain-moving, devil-busting, nothing-is-too-hard-for-my-God kind of faith. As the Lord began to take me through His healing process, I realized that I had lost all confidence in myself and in God's ability to work through me. I didn't even know if I was called to preach or not. It was hard to know what God had deposited in my spirit and what was the wisdom and opinion of men. During that season of forgiving and releasing, the Lord took me to a place of emptying out. I was so fed up with religion and people that it was not too difficult to let go of any aspiration for ministry or anything else that had to do with people.

There is no way to doubt you without also doubting God. God has spoken some very definite things about who you are in the kingdom, as well as your purpose. There are no ifs, buts or maybes. "Forever O Lord, Thy Word is settled in heaven" (Ps. 119:89). It is imperative that we protect our hearing. How we function in the kingdom and the realm of authority that we exercise is the direct result of "what" we know and believe about our purpose.

When Jezebel sent that word to Elijah, she provoked doubt, fear and unbelief in his heart and mind. In essence, she was saying, "I know what God did **to** the prophets of Baal. I know what He accomplished **through** you. Don't you dare think or believe that He will do a miracle **for** you." Her threats were so powerful that Elijah forgot all that had been accomplished on Mt. Caramel, ran for his life and wished to die (1 Kings 19:4). The spirit of Jezebel's influence in the realm of self-doubt manifests itself through failure to properly assess your worth in the kingdom of God. As the righteousness of God, He will go to great length to protect His investment in you.

In order for doubt to be present, there must have first been faith. For example, suppose you had personal knowledge of a financial inheritance that I received. Because of your personal knowledge of this transaction, you now believe I have some money. Six months later you find yourself in a financial crisis, and decide to ask me for a loan. You believe I have the money. You believe your relationship with me is in good standing. You decide to make your request based on an assurance that my answer will be "Yes."

The night before you are prepared to call me, you have a chance meeting with a mutual friend. She tells you that she has heard that I wasted away all of the money. Secondly, she remembers that I didn't really care for you enough to make such a loan, challenging your conviction. She has just successfully planted seeds of doubt, which yield the fruit of unbelief. In its simplest form, spiritual witchcraft is at work, influencing you to doubt without substantiated proof what you originally believed.

Locked up within our God-given "free will" is the expressed desire of the Father that we choose Him. He delights in our choice to be owned by Him. Being under the influence of Jezebel is a direct assault on that decision-making process. The spirit of Jezebel operates very much as a ventriloquist. It is never direct or open in its approach. 1 Kings 19:2 says, "Then Jezebel sent a messenger unto Elijah, saying...." It searches out voices and mindsets that can be used to propagate its will and its objectives. Remember, there can be no Jezebel without Ahab. Very rarely do we deal directly with the spirit of Jezebel. The spirit of Jezebel is proficient at using the voice of reason, logic and human intelligence to oppose the Word of God, generating doubt and unbelief.

For example, the Lord will put it in our heart to go to the nations, but our closest friend will say, "But what about your job?" indicating that God does not know that you work. Another example: you have the gift of healing, but you are sick, and therefore reason, "How can I pray for others to be healed?" Perhaps you find it very difficult to say, "I am called to the office of apostle or prophet, or evangelist, or pastor or teacher." With a sense of false humility, we quote Scripture.

The Bible says, "Do not think of yourself more highly than you ought to think," and we know that is true. Being able to say who you are in the Body is only repeating what God thinks of you. It also says do not think **more** highly, as opposed to do not think highly. "For I say, through the grace given unto me, to every man that is among you, not to think of himself more highly than he ought to think; but to think soberly, according as God hath dealt to every man the measure of faith" (Rom. 12:3). What liberty came to my life when I allowed that to sink in. Selah!

Unbelief

The Israelites wandered around in the wilderness for forty years because of unbelief. Our entire Christian experience is founded upon what we believe. Isaiah asks the question, "Who hath believed the report of the Lord?" I believe the report of the Lord. God is not up in heaven deciding what to do with you on a daily basis. Before the foundation of the world, He chose you. Before your mother met your father or your ancestors migrated, the report of the Lord was written. Jesus said, "Only believe." You do not need to invent what to believe. Through the ages, through 30 or more authors and 66 books of the

Bible, God lays out for us what we are to believe. After the death, burial and resurrection of Jesus, God gave us the indwelling presence of the Holy Spirit to teach us what and how to believe.

We do not fully understand the impact of negative words or the impact of allowing what people say about us to outweigh what God has said about us. As I stated earlier, I was raised a Methodist. During my teenage years, I had a critical encounter with my pastor. I was very tender towards the Lord, and I later learned that I had a keen sensitivity to the Spirit of God. Three events occurred in one year that would take 25 years to overcome. I include this part of my personal testimony to illustrate the importance of words.

First, I was asked to address the congregation with a speech for our annual youth service. The Scripture reading, offering and musical selections were performed by the youth of the church, and I was the speaker. There are certain phrases, terms and words used in Pentecostal circles that were not a part of the everyday language of Methodist believers. Upon my arrival, I was ushered into the women's choir members' dressing room. I was told to wait there until it was my turn to speak. Instinctively, I prayed during that time about what I should share. I took my place on the rostrum (the side reserved for women), and without a script of any kind; I shared from my heart God's concern for how people lived their everyday lives. I specifically remember upbraiding them for conduct during the week that was hypocritical to what they professed on Sunday mornings.

I can only summarize that the many trips I took with my grandmother into Holiness circles had left their imprint on my spirit. The things I shared that morning came to me from somewhere beyond my knowledge. The congregation was left in shock. The women cried and said hearty amens. The men were speechless. We had one minister (female), who encouraged me. I know now that she recognized the call of God on my life. From that time forward, she would often express a personal interest in my spiritual life.

The second occasion was a women's day service, where a woman preached the morning message. This was not the norm, and she even used the side of the pulpit reserved for the men. She was from Washington, DC, and I had never seen anyone like her before. The only female minister I knew was relegated to reading the Scripture on Sunday mornings from the special side for women. I was mesmerized and totally engulfed in what was unfolding before me. As I sat about mid-way in the sanctuary, I heard a voice coming from behind me. The voice said, "Someday you will be just like her." I turned to see who had spoken, but there was no one there. I will never forget the feeling of that experience.

The third occasion was the day I joined the church. It was a normal Sunday and an ordinary service. At the end of the sermon, the pastor gave the invitation to join the church. I, along with three or four others, stood and went forward. Normally, you would stand before the altar until the secretary came and recorded your name. Then, the pastor would come down and shake your hand. Next, a deacon would escort you to a side room where you would be given your offering envelopes and would fill out a pledge card.

Well, there has never been anything routine about my life. That Sunday morning when I reached the front of the church, I fell on my knees at the altar and began sobbing uncontrollably. I could be heard all over the church, weeping as if I had lost my only friend. I took everyone by surprise, and no one knew what to do. Finally, someone lifted me up and escorted me to the side room.

All of these experiences converged on my emotions and provoked me to seek a private audience with the pastor. We went into his study, and I asked the right question to the wrong person. I said, "How do you know when you are called to preach?" He replied, "Oh you don't have to worry about that. God doesn't call women to preach." And with that, I was excused and ushered out the door. I thought, "Well, he would surely know about these things," and dismissed the whole notion – a notion, that would return with a haunting vengeance.

I don't hold any malice toward that minister. I do believe that, had I received a different answer then, perhaps I would not have spent so much time later resisting that call. That is something I will never know for sure, but I do know that lives are shaped by the words that we speak. A seed of doubt had been planted. Right questions need to be asked to the right person in order to get a right answer. Selah. "Why am I here?" and "What is my purpose?" are right questions. God is the only person who can answer them. He created you and only He knows what was in His mind when He shaped and fashioned you.

It does not bring glory to God for us to speak or be less than whom He has made us. True humility is a heart understanding of who we are in light of who He is. Just as I cannot be proud of who I am by comparing myself to you (e.g., the Pharisee in Luke 18:11), I cannot be humble by that comparison either. My humble heart and attitude must be the fruit of knowing how great, awesome and majestic He is. True humility does not produce self-doubt, but rather the bold acclaim of the apostle Paul, "I am what I am by the grace of God" (1 Cor. 15:10). I am called because God called me, and not because you believe I'm called. I will do great exploits for Him because of who He is, and not because of what others are able to see. If I live by faith and not by what I see, why should what others don't see influence me? Therefore, I don't receive the report of the enemy through any human being.

Landmark: Are there any people in your life who consistently tell you what you can't do? Do the people you allow to speak into your life push or hinder you in fulfilling your purpose? Are there things that God shared with you that you have come to doubt? Are you fully persuaded that God can and will bring to pass the prophetic utterances over your life?

Barriers: False humility and low self-esteem. Not knowing your purpose in the kingdom. Not studying the Word of God. Looking to people instead of God to find out your purpose.

Solution: Make a commitment to seek God about your purpose. Make a distinction between knowing your purpose and feeling that you are the one to make it happen. Embrace what God has for you. Give your purpose in the kingdom the proper value. Do not accept from people words that do not bear witness with your spirit. Do not be afraid to be confrontational when people insist on speaking negatively about you or over you. Slay any and all doubt with the progressive revelation of "Christ in you the hope of Glory" (Col. 1:27).

Prayer: Father, I can do all things through Christ Who strengthens me. Thank You Lord, for added strength. Lord, I admit my need of You. I pray today that You will increase my faith. Lord, I actively resist all spirits of doubt, unbelief and fear. Satan, you have no place in my life. I resist you and you must flee. Holy Spirit, I come into agreement with all the counsel of the Godhead. I will be who God has called me to be. Lord, I thank You for planting me and causing me to abound in every good work. Help me to gird up the loins of my mind. In Jesus' Name, and by the power of the Blood, I break every word curse that has been spoken over my life. Lord, I ask You to let every seed of doubt die in the ground, bearing no fruit. If there is anything that has caused me to shrink back from walking in complete liberty, I ask You to expose it and give me the grace and the wisdom to know how to come out from under it in Jesus' Name. Help me to get over the words that have been spoken in my life that have robbed me of my destiny in You. I go all the way back to my childhood, and I free myself from the opinions of men. I am Your servant, Lord, created for good works in Christ and for Your pleasure. I abandon myself to You, in Jesus' Name, Amen.

Scripture Helps: Matthew 13, 14, 15, 17, 21; Mark 5, 6, 9, 11 16; Luke 8; Romans 3, 4, 11; Hebrews 3, 4.

Chapter Nine

So What!

Forgiveness

Not being able to forgive and forget is something with which we all struggle at some point in our lives. For the victims of spiritual witchcraft, unforgiveness can very easily grow from being a barrier into being a stronghold. It is the weapon whereby Satan holds us hostage. Not only will unforgiveness keep you forever the victim, but it also brings growth in every area of your spiritual life to a grinding halt. Matthew 6:14 says, "For if you forgive men their trespasses (that is, their reckless and willful sins, leaving them, letting them go and giving up resentment), your heavenly Father will also forgive you." This reveals to us the heart of our Father on the subject of forgiveness and sets in place His expectation for those who proclaim sonship. Once again, we are confronted with the role that "choice" plays in all of this. "Letting them go and giving up resentment" is something you must choose to do.

In the beginning, you might have to forgive that person, church, denomination or yourself daily. Matthew 18:21,22 says, "Then came Peter to him, and said, Lord, how oft shall my brother sin against me, and I forgive him? Till seven times? Jesus saith unto him, I say not unto thee, until seven times: but, until seventy times seven." Faithfully practicing forgiveness will propel you into a freedom of spirit that will astound you. 2 Corinthians 2:10-11 (Amplified) says, "If you forgive anyone for anything, I too forgive that one; and what I have forgiven, if I have forgiven anything, has been for your sakes in the presence [and with the approval] of Christ, the Messiah, to keep Satan from getting the advantage over us; for we are not ignorant of his wiles and intentions." So, not only do we practice forgiveness in order to be forgiven, but also because it keeps Satan from getting an open door to our spiritual lives.

I remember very vividly when I came face to face with my own unwillingness to forgive my natural father. I was abused as a teenage girl, and after receiving Christ as my personal Savior I still had a very hard time letting go of the pain. I just could not get past the "how" questions. "How could he do this to his own flesh and blood?" and "How could God allow this?" and "How could my mother and grandparents turn their heads and act as if they didn't know what was happening to me?" and on and on. It took a long time for my pastor's wife to be able to get past my defenses, but finally she was able to help me face the truth. It had happened, and if I was going to be saved and free, I had to forgive. I had to choose to forgive. It was the hardest thing I have ever done. What concerned me the most was that no one had ever validated for me that I had indeed been wronged. It seemed inconceivable to me that I should forgive a wrong when no one was willing to admit that a wrong had been committed.

By the time I reached the point of needing to forgive my ex-pastors and other leaders, it was much easier. The victory that I had received in this earlier battle gave me access to the grace needed for the occasions that followed. I've always been stubborn. That stubbornness began to pay off for me in a positive way. I was not going to let anyone or anything stand in the way of my pursuit to be totally free. I rehearsed conversations and emotions, bringing up faces and places in my mind's eye until I had forgiven everybody for everything. I was determined to "GET OVER" the things I had suffered and get over I did. You too can "GET OVER" every victimizing experience. "You can do all things through Christ who strengthens you" (Phil. 4:13).

Let It Go

In 1994, I was visiting a friend's church in Philadelphia. I had just come through a really tough battle. I needed the strength of corporate worship to help me get over my latest challenge. I had been asked to lead the worship and had been able to go past my pain to usher us into God's presence. When I handed the microphone to the guest minister, he was encouraged to follow the leading of the Holy Ghost. I somehow knew that I was going to receive some prophetic ministry, so I braced myself.

Over the years, I have received ministry from all types of gifting, but I was not prepared for what happened next. He ministered quite a few things, into all of which I won't go here. At the end of his ministry to me, he began to yell at me. He looked me right in the eyes and shouted, "So what, he left you; so what, it wasn't right; SO WHAT! I am here, says the Lord. I AM HERE!"

Well, something broke in me from such a deep place I didn't even know was there. A root of rejection had been pulled up with the words, "So what!" I laugh now, because I understand that there are some things that happen to us that all you can do is say, "So what," and go on. It is not a question of "who, what, when, where or how." It is a question of letting it go. It is a matter of forgiving and forgetting.

"Acquit" is a legal term. It means to let go, to pardon, to release from guilt. Maybe you can remember having this happen to you. I know I can. Someone has done something to hurt you. You are holding a grudge, refusing to forget about it. You run into that person sometime later. They speak to you as though nothing bad or wrong has ever occurred. You are miserable, but they are happy-go-lucky. You are holding on to it, and therefore, it is holding on to you. There can be no letting go from the influence of spiritual witchcraft until we let go of how we are connected to it. This is the power that God is trying to reveal to us in our quest to be free – the power that is locked up in what I call the spirit of release.

During a season in my life, I was required to let go of people and things. Much like Job, one after another things and people were taken from my life. I was under direct order of the Holy Spirit not to fight back or defend myself in any way. I came to a place where literally all I could do was lie on the floor and cry. I was saying to God, "I love You, but I don't understand this. I love You, Lord, but You are killing me." It was only after I had received healing that the Lord spoke to me that I had learned the spirit of release. Actually, it was another type of dying. I had come into a place of total surrender. No matter what He required, I would hold nothing more dearly than Him.

Until we acquit, pardon and release those who have hurt us, misused us and abused us, we will not be free. As long as we hold on to it, it will hold on to us. Acquittal is not about determining guilt or innocence. It is a conscious decision to release the guilty party. It is over, it is done, and it is finished.

Landmark: I believe it would be safe to say here that this book is one more tool in God's arsenal to help those victimized by spiritual witchcraft to be free. The Spirit of God is saying to you as you are reading this book, "YES, you have been victimized, but forgive. Let it go; let the person go; let that denomination or religion or spiritual leader go. Choose now to forgive. Let the bitterness go." "Forgetting those things which are behind and reaching forth unto those things which are before..." (Phil. 3:13). There is so much before you. His purpose and destiny await you. Are you bitter? Are there any people you know whom you have not forgiven? As you were reading this chapter, did people come to your mind? Are you being honest with yourself?

Barriers: Stubbornness, a judgmental spirit and pride will hold you hostage. Not forgetting and refusing to let go of the past. Living in the past. Expecting your future to be the same as your past experiences. Not believing that God is greater than your past.

Solution: Cut the spirit of Jezebel off at the knees by forgiving. Let it all go. Every word that was ever spoken contrary to what God has said concerning you can die in the ground by your decision to forgive the person who said it. You can close every door of access to the enemy by refusing to become bitter. Over the next few days, the Lord will bring the faces of people before your mind's eye. Forgive each one. Whenever you start to remember past conversations, release that person by saying out aloud, "I choose to forgive you." You might not feel any different at first, but saying the words out aloud releases the Holy Spirit to do the work. He will thoroughly remove any unforgiveness from your heart and mind, enabling you to also forget.

Prayer: Lord, I choose to forgive all those who have offended me. Father, I forgive all those who have manipulated me or controlled me. I ask You to forgive me for holding any unforgiveness or bitterness in my heart, and I forgive myself. Lord, I choose to release and acquit all who have wounded me in any way. Holy Spirit, search my heart and reveal any areas of bitterness, unforgiveness and hostility. Show me if I am being stubborn or prideful in any way. Help me, Lord, to be able to empty out before You. Father, give me the grace that I need to be able to walk in love. I pray for those who have despitefully used me, and I bless those who have cursed me. Give me a heart change, and teach me how to love my enemies. I ask You now to give me peace and to let your Spirit fill my very being. Holy Spirit, heal my heart, soul and mind and make me whole, in Jesus' Name, Amen.

Scripture Helps: Genesis 50, Psalms 25, 86; Proverbs 11, 16, 29; Matthew 5, 6, 7, 18; Mark 11; Luke 6, 11, 17; 2 Corinthians 2; Acts 8; Ephesians 4; Hebrews 12.

SECTION THREE

Chapter Ten

Moving Out of Religion and Into Relationship

Religion

AReligious spirit works through a mindset or the "way" a person thinks, often marked by inflexibility. Denominations, legalism, traditions, dogmas are expressions of a Religious spirit. During those 18 years of service to a religious denomination, I practiced religion diligently. I promised to share some of those rules, so here they are:

- Wearing earrings, sandals, pants, short sleeves, and make-up were all forbidden.

- Going to the movies, bowling, skating or any type of "worldly" activity was forbidden.

- If divorced and remarried, forbidden to hold an office in the church, yet allowed to pay reports.

- Use of any translation other than King James was forbidden.

- Listening to any music other than gospel was forbidden.

- Going to hear preachers not in the denomination was forbidden.

One of the dangers with adhering to this type of list is that most of it deals with the external or outer aspect of our Christian walk. We were so busy looking saved and presenting a certain image that not nearly enough attention was given to the weightier matters. Things such as backbiting, gossip, envy, jealousy, pride and self-righteousness were often left unchecked. Jesus addresses this very issue in Matthew 23:24-29.

Ye blind guides, which strain at a gnat, and swallow a camel. Woe unto you, scribes and Pharisees, hypocrites! For ye make clean the outside of the cup and of the platter, but within they are full of extortion and excess. Thou blind Pharisee, cleanse first that which is within the cup and platter, that the outside of them may be clean also. Woe unto you, scribes and Pharisees, hypocrites! For ye are like unto whited sepulchres, which indeed appear beautiful outward, but are within full of dead men's bones, and of all uncleanness. Even so ye also outwardly appear righteous unto men, but within ye are full of hypocrisy and iniquity. Woe unto you, scribes and Pharisees, hypocrites! Because ye build the tombs of the prophets, and garnish the sepulchres of the righteous,

A spirit of condemnation was our taskmaster. Instead of living a sanctified life produced by my great love for him, I was living a life full of fear. I did not have the revelation of my righteousness being fully accomplished through the atoning death of Christ. "For He hath made Him to be sin for us, who knew no sin; that we might be made the righteousness of God in Him" (2 Cor. 5:21). "In Him," is the difference between religion and relationship. Religion focuses on what is "in me," while relationship is dependent upon being "in Him." Relationship with Him is the only thing that will change what is in me. Relationship with Him will change what and how I practice.

This is the very dilemma that makes the spirit of Jezebel so dangerous and damaging. The spirit of Jezebel relentlessly presents relationships and emotional attachments as substitutes for intimacy with the Father. All of our relationships within the Body of Christ should point us to the headship of Jesus. Without regard to titles, mantles, etc., we all have the same charge with regard to fellow believers. Jesus said to Peter, "But I have prayed for thee, that thy faith fail not: when thou art converted, strengthen thy brother" (Luke 22:32). The ministry of restoration is given to the spiritual not the religious (Gal. 6:1). Spirituality is the fruit of intimacy and not the result of blind adherence to religious practices.

Near the end of my time with the denomination, I became very frustrated and quite dissatisfied. This produced a kind of boldness, which was identified by my pastor as rebellion. I showed up for one service with make-up and earrings on. After the sermon, I was summoned to the altar. My pastor then proceeded to remove my earrings, placing them in the pocket of her robe. I was publicly humiliated and began to cry. She took this as a sign of repentance, but I was angry because my respect for her would not allow me to do what I really wanted to do. That episode really was the beginning of the end for me.

The presence of a notable double standard was also alarming in those days. We would receive guest ministers who would arrive wearing make-up and jewelry. I questioned how could these persons preach to us doing things that we were forbidden to do? It just did not add up for me. There were other inconsistencies also. In the beginning it was easy to keep these rules. As the years passed it became more difficult, because I could see blatant discrepancies between what we were taught and what leaders actually did. I eventually reached the point where I could no longer teach these rules. My spirit was grieved. I felt trapped and understood that I was enslaving people to a system in which I did not believe. Congregations were being financially plundered, and there was no real concern for the souls of men.

As I look back, I am now able to admit that practicing religion, adhering to and keeping "do's and don'ts," did not sustain me. It did not prevent me from falling into sin. However, after I left that organization, I was able to develop a closer, more intimate relationship with Jesus. The intimacy that came from our growing closer to each other produced a grace in my life that kept me from falling into sin in areas in which I had come to believe I would never get the victory.

The Fruit of Intimacy

To ensure that we are successful survivors of spiritual witchcraft, there is a need to recommit to our relationship with the Lord Jesus Christ. Throughout our quest to be free and our in-depth look at how spiritual witchcraft works, we have discovered the importance of right relationships. The objective of the enemy is to disrupt and/or destroy relationships. Spiritual witchcraft involves the controlling and manipulating of another person's will. The objective of exercising spiritual witchcraft is to gain control. Control was at the heart of what Adam lost in the garden. Through the fall, Satan gained control over the souls of men, forcing separation from God. The atoning work of Christ restored fellowship and provided a vehicle for control to be restored to our spirit man.

I must guard and protect my relationship with the Lord at all cost. When we are born-again, we are making a declaration to ourselves and to the world. We are declaring that Jesus Christ has ownership of our lives. We are making a vow to let Jesus be our Lord and Master. This cannot be accomplished by the keeping of the law. If it could have been accomplished by adhering to a list of "do's and don'ts," then there would have been no need for the Blood sacrifice of Jesus (Heb. 10:19). But, Jesus paid the price of shedding His own Blood to restore us to intimacy with the Father.

Hear these words from the Amplified Bible from Apostle Paul on intimacy (Phil. 3:8-11):

Yes, furthermore, I count everything as loss compared to the possession of the priceless privilege (the overwhelming preciousness, the surpassing worth, and supreme advantage) of knowing Christ Jesus my Lord {and} of progressively becoming more deeply {and} intimately acquainted with Him [of perceiving and recognizing and understanding Him more fully and clearly]. For His sake I have lost everything and consider it all to be mere rubbish (refuse, dregs), in order that I may win (gain) Christ (the Anointed One), And that I may [actually] be found {and} known as in Him, not having any [self-achieved] righteousness that can be called my own, based on my obedience to the Law's demands (ritualistic uprightness and supposed right standing with God thus acquired), but possessing that [genuine righteousness] which comes through faith in Christ (the Anointed One), the [truly] right standing with God, which comes from God by [saving] faith.

[For my determined purpose is] that I may know Him [that I may progressively become more deeply and intimately acquainted with Him, perceiving and recognizing and understanding the wonders of His Person more strongly and more clearly], and that I may in that same way come to know the power outflowing from His resurrection [which it exerts over believers], and that I may so share His sufferings as to be continually transformed [in spirit into His likeness even] to His death, [in the hope] That if possible I may attain to the [spiritual and moral] resurrection [that lifts me] out from among the dead [even while in the body].

The Apostle Paul articulated a hunger for God that was marked by a hunger for intimacy with God. As I was studying this particular subject for a course I was teaching I received some personal insights I would like to share with you. Performing intimate acts does not guarantee that the person performing the act is being truly intimate. Secondly, knowing intimate phrases doesn't guarantee true intimacy. Prostitutes do intimate acts without being intimately involved. In order for true intimacy to exist between two individuals, there must be an involvement of their entire beings. If we are to have intimacy with our Abba Father, we must be willing to come before Him in total honesty. We must allow Him access to our spirits, souls and bodies.

The fruit of intimacy is a desire to give the highest place of priority to my relationship with the Lord. What He has said must outweigh what any other person or spirit, including me, has to say. What He thinks becomes the guide for living my life. What He expects and requires of me, what He purposes for me, serves as an anchor for my relationship with Him. There can be no freedom from spiritual witchcraft without true ownership by the Lord. He must be Lord indeed.

During this season, the Body of Christ is filled with an expectation of the outpouring of the Glory of God. Paramount to experiencing a breaking out of signs, wonders and miracles, we must cultivate an intimate relationship with Jesus that supersedes every other relationship in our life. Just as Moses forsook all to dwell on the mountain with Jehovah, we must cling to Jesus, allowing our fellowship with Him to produce a vehicle through which He can pour forth His glory. The Apostle Paul said, "For my determined purpose is...." This is the hunger that God is restoring to His Body, a hunger for a relationship with Him that is so intimate that we are impregnated with a vision. Deep is calling to deep. You must respond by becoming as free as possible. The people who know their God shall do great exploits.

If you wanted to get to know me better, you would have to spend time with me. You could talk to my daughters, interview other family members and friends. They all would be able to tell you things about me. At this point you would know things about me, but you would not be able to say you know me until you receive first-hand knowledge of me. This could not be accomplished in a few hours. You would need to see me in different types of settings and circumstances to really know me. The Bible is a compilation of circumstances and situations that reveal to us who God is through the eyes of others. Jesus and the Father are one. Jesus said, "He that hath seen Me hath seen the Father" (John 14:9). You must allow the Holy Spirit to reveal to you who Jesus is. Knowledge that is acquired in this fashion is not easily shaken. In other words, there are things that I know about God through study and experience that no one can take away from me. This knowledge becomes an awesome weapon in the life of a believer.

Landmark: Are you attempting to work out your salvation by adhering to a list of do's and don'ts? Do you submit to religious spirits operating through others? What is the fruit in your life that proves God's ownership of you? Who in your life is insistent on telling you how to be with your Abba Father? What have you said or done to give them the impression that it is OK for them to dictate how you interact with your Father? Do you tolerate this interference? Why? How much of what you know about God is the direct result of your own pursuit to know Him?

Barriers: Letting tradition and the doctrines of men have more importance than the Word of God. Esteeming religious leaders more highly than you should. Not standing up for your right to have a personal relationship with Jesus. Being fearful of intimacy with Jesus.

Solution: The only way to replace religion with an intimate relationship is to spend time in God's presence. This is accomplished through spending time in prayer, studying and meditating on the Word of God, spending time praising and worshipping God, and spending time sitting quietly before the Lord, allowing Him the freedom to speak to you. There is no shortcut. No one else can do it for you. Challenge yourself in this way, keep a log of how much time you spend with the Father in the course of one week.

Prayer: Father, I come to You in the precious Name of Jesus. I thank You Lord for all that You are doing in my life. I give You praise for the opportunity to know You personally. Lord, I confess my sins to You, and I ask You to forgive me. Lord, my desire is to be free indeed. Holy Spirit, show me areas where religious spirits instead of the Living God are controlling me. Reveal Jesus to me, I want to know Him more intimately. Give me a hunger for the Word of God. Grant me sweet times of refreshing and communion in His presence. Open up my understanding of Your Word more fully, in Jesus' Name. I ask for divine wisdom from above. Lord, bless me indeed, enlarge my borders, go with me and keep me from evil, in Jesus' Name I pray, Amen.

Scripture Helps: Psalm 50, 51, 119; Jeremiah 31; Micah 6; Matthew 7, 15, 19, 23; Mark 10; Luke 22; Romans 4, 5, 8, 10; 2 Corinthians 3; Ephesians 2; Hebrews 8, 9, 10.

Chapter Eleven

Getting On

This Won't Hurt at All

You are sitting in the doctor's office. You've had your examination and you are now waiting for the nurse. She opens the door and walks toward you with a three-inch needle in her hand. She looks you in the eyes, and seeing your concern, she responds, "Oh, this won't hurt a bit, just a pinch." But, it's a tetanus shot. What she should have said is that the pain won't last too long. There is going to be pain.

Consider this: By the time an expectant woman reaches the end of her pregnancy, she is miserable. She wants the baby out of her body. Even though she realizes that means going into labor, she longs to have her body back. During the labor she might do many embarrassing things because of the pain. During my daughter's labor, a critical point was reached. She had been in labor about 16 hours and was near the end. During one of her contractions, she looked over at me in such earnest and said, "I can't do this." Her statement took me totally by surprise. I was thinking to myself, "You should have considered that when you were conceiving this blessing from the Lord." Fortunately, my motherly instincts took over and I responded, "But honey you are already doing it. It's just about over." She was so engrossed in the pushing and panting and surviving the pain that she was not aware of how far she had come or how close she was to delivery.

Now, you may be at a place in your quest to be free and so involved in the surviving that you may not be able even to see the progress you have made. Progress is being made. You will never be the same. Nor will anyone be able to misuse or abuse you again. You will gain a new respect for right leadership and sensitivity to those who are in bondage to spiritual witchcraft. Just like our expectant mother, in the end, you will rejoice. Yes, she will have new responsibilities. There will be midnight feedings and dirty diapers. Her life will undergo a total upheaval, but her body will once again be her own.

Spiritual witchcraft feeds on intimacy, trust, confidence and closeness. Desiring to be free will produce pain. Taking steps to be free will no doubt bring pain. You will have bouts with loneliness, rejection and depression. Even though it was **your** decision to be free, you will feel rejected. This is partially due to the fact that your mind will still be attempting to figure out or justify what you have been through. You will be tempted to try and "fix" things between you and your abuser. You will need to remember that you are not the only one exercising "choice" in this situation.

The person who was controlling or manipulating you was also choosing. Their choice was to have their own way at the expense of overriding your will. At this critical junction in your quest to be free, "draw nigh to Him; He will draw nigh to you" (James 4:8). Not only will He stop the pain, heal the hurt, but also He will move into that empty place, "and there is a friend that sticketh closer than a brother" (Prov. 18:24). At the appointed time, He will restore everything you need in the area of relationships.

Returning ownership of our hearts and minds to God and living in the freedom that has been appropriated for us is the ultimate goal in our quest to be free. As we go through the last stages, I want to make some distinctions between the types of pain you will experience. When you are **getting out** of abusive, controlling, manipulative relationships, you experience pain that is mingled with shock, frustration and anger. So much "truth" is invading your thought life that you are reeling. In your mind and heart, you will feel like you are on a roller coaster. You will remember with great fondness situations and events. Then "truth" will raise its head, and pain will shoot through your heart. As you resolve yourself to leave or sever the relationship in obedience to God, this pain will cease. We will endure the intense pain, knowing that it will not last forever and that anything we suffer here is not "worthy to be compared to the glory which shall be revealed in us" (Rom. 8:18).

Hold Still

The second type of pain you will deal with is the pain produced from **letting go.** This dull, aching pain is similar to grieving over the death of a loved one. The problem is, the person is still alive. It would be easier in some ways if they had died. Your decision to move on with God has required this letting go. You will fret over the "what ifs," but you must keep things in perspective. The fruit of intimacy with Jesus is being able to be totally honest with Him. You can be where you are. He is touched with the feelings of our infirmities. There is no need to pretend. Pour out your heart to Him.

Back to the doctor's office for a minute.... You have seen the needle. You heard what the nurse had to say, but you know better. After all, you are not 3 or 4 years old. It is going to hurt. The nurse knows you know better. Her next command is, "Hold still! I am going to stick you, but be still. Let's get this over with." Any attempt to run away rather than confront the situation will have a disastrous end. You came to get the needle. You need the needle. It is too late to retreat. You might even remind yourself about how you came into this predicament in the first place. Eventually you will pull yourself together and take the shot.

You are too committed to God to succumb to spiritual witchcraft. You received salvation to put God in charge of your life. You might not understand how you got into an abusive spiritual situation, but there is no doubt that you want out of it. Hold still, and let God do His thing. You have done your part, just like our patient in the doctor's office. You made it to the right place. You have allowed the truth of God's Word to bring you into greater light. You have forgiven yourself and others. Now take the antidote. Sit still, letting the love of God flood your being. Quiet your spirit, and still your mind. You can do this. Sometimes the hardest thing for a believer to do is what appears to be "nothing." There are times when nothing is exactly what God desires us to do. It is during those times that obedience becomes the issue. There is nothing you can do in your strength. Even our emotional and mental healing must come from Him. Enter into the rest, His rest.

You did not get into your situation overnight. Becoming free is a process. You must take one step at a time, one day at a time. Depending on our personalities and experiences, our route to recovery may vary. Do not compare yourself to anyone else. Allow the Holy Spirit to lead you in the way that you should go. David said, "He leadeth me besides the still waters" (Ps. 23:2). There is a time to plunge into the river and a time to be led to the still waters that will restore our souls. Being made whole will produce balance and stability.

Breathe In & Breathe Out

Finally, there will be bittersweet pain because of your decision to move on. The pain of letting go will be contradicted by the joy of anticipating the new. You will experience sadness because of the loss of relationships as well as excitement about your future. Just as a person who has lost a spouse feels guilty at the start of a new relationship, you will be tempted to feel guilty about your decision to move on. **Don't.** It is time, and it is God's will.

You have done it. You obeyed the Lord and now you are ready to move on. The apostle Paul said, "His strength is made perfect in weakness" (2 Cor. 12:9). It's not done by might nor by power, but by His Spirit (Zech. 4:6). Let the Spirit of God take you into freedom. Let the breath of the Almighty breathe on you, refreshing and renewing you.

I was present for the birth of all four of my grandchildren. Being an excellent coach, I repeatedly said, "breathe" to each of my daughters. I cannot tell you in medical terminology how that helps to get through the intense pain of childbirth, but it does work. I have been in other tense situations and found that just taking in deep breaths and blowing the air out has a calming effect.

You might be tempted to go into hysteria because of the pain. Feeling overwhelmed as you get close to the end of this journey for greater freedom is normal, but breathe. Breathe in by reading the Word of God. Breathe out by forgiving. Breathe in by praying in the spirit. Breathe out by making your faith confessions. Breathe in by maintaining fellowship with the saints. Breathe out by separating yourself from the abuser or abusive situation. Breathe in by speaking out loud the purpose of God for your life. Breathe out by vocally declaring your intention to be used only by the Holy Spirit. Breathe in by seeking Him, by lying in His presence. Breathe out by watching what you allow to be spoken into your spirit. Breathe in by worshipping. Breathe out by refusing to speak negatively about yourself or others.

"Weeping may endure for a night, but joy cometh in the morning" (Ps. 30:5). It will soon be over, just a memory, but you will have a new baby. When you come out on the other side of the pain, you will have renewed or new purpose, new relationships, a new ministry or a new beginning. Keep your eyes on the Lord. "Looking unto Jesus the Author and Finisher of our faith; Who for the joy that was set before Him endured the cross, despising the shame, and is set down at the right hand of the throne of God" (Heb. 12:2). Making a new commitment to hear and obey His voice, expect Him to speak to you. Also remember this – if you suffer with Him you will also reign with Him (2 Tim 2:12).

"Count it all joy when you fall into divers temptations; knowing this that the trying of your faith worketh patience" (James 1:3). Whatever has happened to you has been allowed for God's purpose. He never makes a mistake, especially in what He allows. If He allowed it, then it is for your blessing and benefit. God is a master at turning what the enemy has meant for harm into something powerfully good (Rom. 8:28). As you move on, God will begin to reveal how He can use for His glory what you have experienced. Just your testimony alone becomes an effective tool for setting others free. We overcome by the Blood of the Lamb and the word of our testimony (Rev. 12:11).

Looking back over my life, I realize that my survival has been predicated upon a consistent adherence to a particular mindset. In spite of obstacles, difficulties, trials, tests and storms, I have maintained the disposition of no stopping. "KEEP MOVING" has been my motto. As I was attempting to write the last chapter of this book, I hit a stone wall. I just did not seem to be able to write anymore. I could not bring together any more thoughts that would help us in our quest to be free. I was lying before the Lord and meditating on my dilemma, when the Holy Spirit spoke this revelation to me. He said, "Lynda, there is nothing else to write."

Let's review for a minute, and then you will laugh with me. This is the route our quest to be free has taken us. We came **"out"** of the abusive situation. We dealt with our barriers. We have come to terms with what happened to us. We have truly been healed and are **"over"** it. We have released everyone from everything. To further quote the Holy Spirit, "There really isn't any thing else to do, except to MOVE ON. Get on. Get on with your life. Get on with your purpose. Fulfill your destiny. Move on into that new relationship, new church, and new ministry. Move on through that next door of opportunity. Move on in Jesus' Name. AMEN!

Scripture Helps: Nehemiah 6; Job 23; Psalm 116; Habakkuk 2; John 16; 2 Corinthians 1; Galatians 5; 2 Timothy 1, 2, 3, 4; 1 John 5; Jude; Revelation 2.

Chapter Twelve

Stand Fast

IN [THIS] freedom Christ has made us free – completely liberated us; stand fast then, and do not be hampered and held ensnared and submit again to a yoke of slavery – which you have once put off.
Galatians 5:1 Amplified

God has made a way for us to continue in freedom. We must continue to choose day-by-day, hour-by-hour and moment-by-moment to stand our ground. I choose to walk in the liberty that Christ has given me. Without regard to how often I am confronted with controlling, manipulative, seducing, witchcraft spirits I choose to say **"NO, NOT TODAY DEVIL!"** I would love to be able to tell you that once you have come through your ordeal, you won't have to deal with these spirits again, but I can't. I can share with you some observations as a result of continuing to fight these oppressive spirits that will help in your battle to stay free.

- It takes less and less time to recognize abusive or potentially abusive situations.

- You will experience less trauma each time, when faced with a controlling or manipulative relationship that needs to be ended.

- You will take each encounter less personally. It is not about you, but about the enemy who desires to have you abort the purposes of God for your life.

- Spirits of control, fear, intimidation and manipulation can operate very subtlety and do not like to be challenged.

- You do not have to succumb to these spirits to be accepted in the Beloved.

- There is power in your tongue. When you speak forth the purposes of God for your life, you upset these spirits.

- When you make open declarations affirming your decision not to be used by any other spirit, the spirit of Jezebel is offended and will leave your presence.

- Allow the Holy Spirit free reign in your relationships from the start. It is easier to accept His wisdom at the onset than to try to get out of situations that are potentially enslaving.

Review

1. Ask the Holy Spirit to reveal any relationships that do not line up with the Word of God. Be thorough.

2. Admit to yourself the truth of the presence of any controlling, manipulating relationships.

3. Take the necessary steps to get out of any and all spiritually abusive situations.

4. Cut every soul tie through prayer.

5. Deal with your barriers and issues honestly. Lay it all out before God. Do not try to justify how you feel. Confess your feelings and allow God to heal you.

6. Forgive yourself and all those who have wounded or offended you.

7. Get over your experience by releasing and acquitting all guilty parties.

8. Build yourself up by reading the Word of God. Pray for new revelation and the grace to empty out all pre-conceived ideas in order to receive the new.

9. Through worship, get into the presence of God, seeking His direction in order to move on.

10. Once you are sure you know God's will, obey Him.

11. Share your testimony with others.

Other Books Available
from Lighthouse Publications

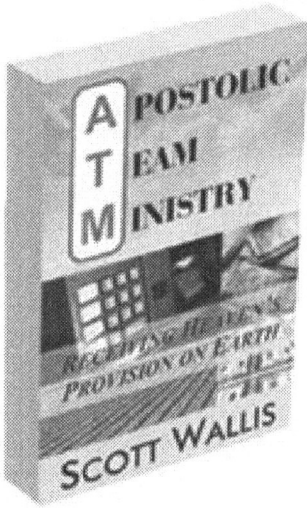

Apostolic Team Ministry

Pastor/Prophet Scott Wallis provides practical answers to the questions that many believers have, such as: "How can I overcome lack in my life?" Learn why apostles are so important to the purpose and plans of God, and how apostolic teams release tremendous supernatural power and wealth into the Church.

Author: Scott Wallis
Retail Price: $11.99
ISBN: 0964221128

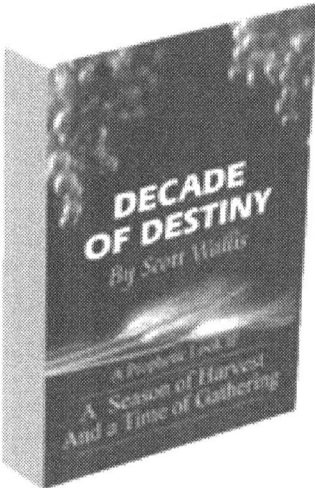

Decade of Destiny

A powerful prophetic word detailing what God is doing in our days. First written in 1991, this timeless book has proven to be an accurate window into the future. Discover what God is saying to His Church today!

Author: Scott Wallis
Retail Price: $11.99
ISBN: 0964221195

183

The Third Reformation is Coming

Prophetic leaders have been declaring for several years that a third reformational movement of the Holy Spirit was about to begin. Find out what this third reformation is and how it will radically change the Church and your life.

Author: Scott Wallis
Retail Price: $9.99
ISBN: 0964221144

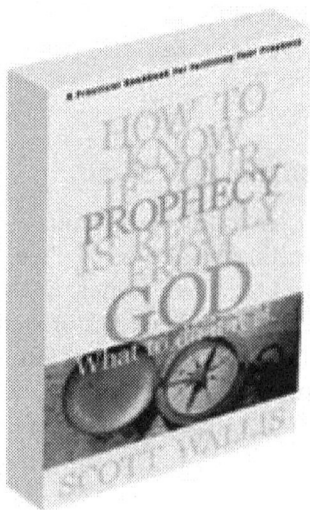

How to Know if Your Prophecy is Really from God

One of the most important books on prophecy available for Believers. If you have ever received a prophetic word, then this book will help you discern if that word was from God, and if it was, what to do with it to see if fulfilled.

Author: Scott Wallis
Retail Price: $11.99
ISBN: 1931232415

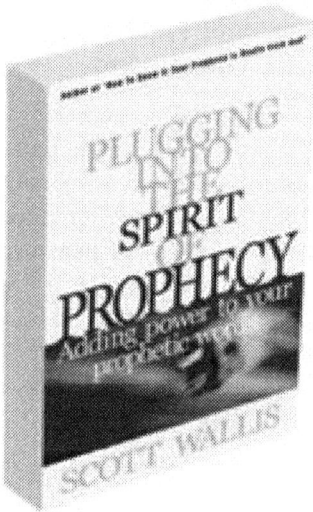

Plugging into the Spirit of Prophecy

God has designed every believer to walk in the prophetic. You can learn how to flow in the Holy Spirit of prophecy. This exciting book will teach you how to do this and more. You will experience God's awesome power through the prophetic word.

Author: Scott Wallis
Retail Price: $11.99
ISBN: 1931232210

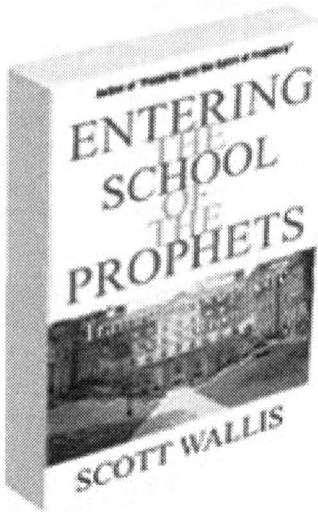

Entering the School of the Prophets

Scott Wallis's third book in his series on understanding prophetic ministry that answers questions regarding the prophetic office and its value to the Body of Christ today. A great resource for those desiring to understand more about the prophetic office and ministry.

Author: Scott Wallis
Retail Price: $12.99
ISBN: 1-933656-04-2

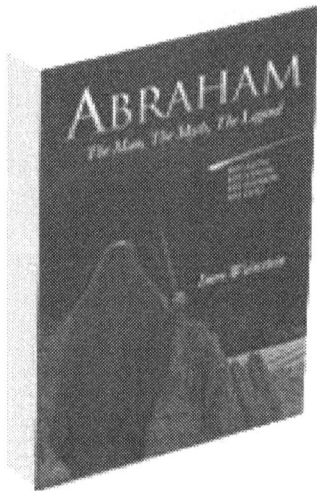

Abraham: The Man, The Myth, The Legend

A fictional account of Abraham's early years, based in a Biblical worldview. All the wonder of God's redemption in the life of a young pagan man, his glorious romance with Sarai, the exciting action of battles and rescue encounters, and his discovery of the one true God of the universe.

Authors: Imre Weinstein
Retail Price: $19.99
Pre-Order Price: $13.99
ISBN: 1933656018

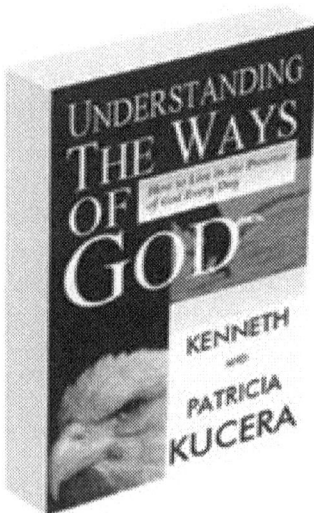

Understanding the Ways of God

You can understand the mysteries behind God's ways. No longer wonder why God does what He does – you can know. As you read this exciting book, you will learn secret after secret of walking in the ways of God. Unlock the potential God has placed inside of you as you learn the ways of God!

Authors: Ken & Pat Kucera
Retail Price: $11.99
ISBN: 0964221152

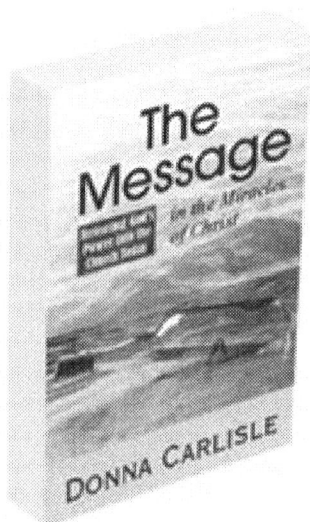

The Message in the Miracles of Christ

Recently, researchers have discovered that there may be hidden coded messages in the actual text of the Bible. Could it be that the miracles of Jesus also reveal hidden messages of what God is doing in our day? Discover the answer as you read this exciting book!

Author: Donna Carlisle
Retail Price: $14.99
ISBN: 0964221136

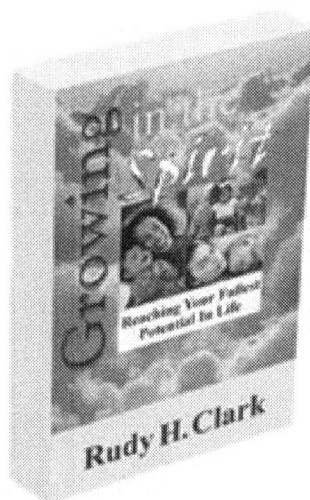

Growing in the Spirit

Taking from life examples, Pastor/Prophet Rudy Clark reveals principles of spiritual growth. Through many life lessons, God has taught Reverend Clark the values and virtues that have made him the man he is today. Experience freedom as you learn how to reach your fullest potential.

Author: Rudy H. Clark
Retail Price: $14.99
ISBN: 0964221160

187

These and other Christian books from Lighthouse Publications are available at participating local Christian bookstores, Amazon.com & Bn.com.

To order books directly from
Lighthouse Publications,
visit www.Lighthouse-Publications.com

Lighthouse Publications
2028 Larkin Avenue
Elgin, IL 60123
(847) 697-6788